FOREIGN POLICY ASSOCIATION
Headline Series

No. 266 FOREIGN POLICY ASSOCIATION $3.00

THE PUERTO RICAN QUESTION

by Jorge Heine
and Juan M. García-Passalacqua

	Preface	3
1	From Guánica to the New Deal	7
2	The Commonwealth: Politics and Society	17
3	An Economy in Transition	32
4	Puerto Rico on the Global Scene	48
5	A Way Out of the Quandary	56
	Talking It Over	69
	Annotated Reading List	70

Cover Design: Hersch Wartik   November/December 1983

The Authors

JORGE HEINE is director of the Caribbean Institute and Study Center for Latin America (CISCLA) at the Inter-American University of Puerto Rico, San Germán, and will be a visiting fellow at St. Antony's College, Oxford University, in 1984. He was previously a research associate at the Latin American Program of the Woodrow Wilson International Center for Scholars in Washington, D.C. He is the editor and coauthor of *Time for Decision: The United States and Puerto Rico* (1983) and has degrees from the University of Chile Law School, York University, and Stanford University.

JUAN MANUEL GARCÍA-PASSALACQUA is a political analyst for *The San Juan Star*. A former aide to Governors Luis Muñoz Marín and Roberto Sánchez Vilella, he is the author of five books and numerous articles in professional journals. His *Puerto Rico: Equality and Freedom at Issue in the Caribbean* will be published by Praeger in 1984. He holds degrees from the University of Puerto Rico, Tufts and Tulane universities, and Harvard Law School.

This work is dedicated to Norma and Ivonne, compañeras.

The Foreign Policy Association

The Foreign Policy Association is a private, nonprofit, nonpartisan educational organization. Its purpose is to stimulate wider interest and more effective participation in, and greater understanding of, world affairs among American citizens. Among its activities is the continuous publication, dating from 1935, of the HEADLINE SERIES. The authors are responsible for factual accuracy and for the views expressed. FPA itself takes no position on issues of United States foreign policy.

HEADLINE SERIES (ISSN 0017-8780) is published five times a year, January, March, May, September and November, by the Foreign Policy Association, Inc., 205 Lexington Ave., New York, N.Y. 10016. Chairman, Leonard H. Marks; President, Archie E. Albright; Editor, Nancy L. Hoepli; Associate Editors, Ann R. Monjo and Mary E. Stavrou. Subscription rates, $12.00 for 5 issues; $20.00 for 10 issues; $28.00 for 15 issues. Single copy price $3.00. Discount 25% on 10 to 99 copies; 30% on 100 to 499; 35% on 500 to 999; 40% on 1,000 or more. Payment must accompany order for $6 or less. Second-class postage paid at New York, N.Y. POSTMASTER: Send address changes to HEADLINE SERIES, Foreign Policy Association, 205 Lexington Ave., New York, N.Y. 10016. Copyright 1984 by Foreign Policy Association, Inc. Composed and printed at Science Press, Ephrata, Pa.

Library of Congress Catalog No. 84-80499
ISBN 0-87124-088-2

Preface

On the night of January 11, 1981, as the Salvadoran guerrillas engaged in their "final offensive" against the Duarte government, some 1,600 miles east of war-torn El Salvador, 11 jet fighters of Puerto Rico's National Guard, worth $45 million, were blown up near the capital, San Juan. The attack, undertaken by the *Macheteros*—a clandestine group named after the roving bands who fought U.S. troops following the 1898 invasion of Puerto Rico—was a protest against U.S. involvement in El Salvador's civil war. It was also the most spectacular and effective guerrilla attack to take place under the U.S. flag, one of a long series of "armed propaganda actions" undertaken by various Puerto Rican pro-independence groups both on the island and on the U.S. mainland.

Should the United States continue to hold on to Puerto Rico or should the island join the 13 Caribbean nations that have become independent since 1962? Should Puerto Rico's present Commonwealth status, under which Puerto Ricans enjoy U.S. citizenship and have their own elected government but leave all foreign affairs and defense matters in the hands of Washington, be strengthened and expanded? Or, rather, is it only as the 51st state of the Union that Puerto Rico will be able to solve its status dilemma?

> *The preparation and publication of this issue of the* HEADLINE SERIES *was made possible in part by a grant from The Ford Foundation.*

In the 1970s a number of forces were unleashed on the island, in the United States and on the global scene that have given new urgency to the need to resolve the question of Puerto Rico's future status.

Over and beyond violent manifestations of anti-U.S. feelings by small groups at the fringes of Puerto Rican politics, a growing political dissatisfaction among members of all parties with the present Commonwealth ties to the United States has become apparent. Supporters of Puerto Rican independence have never accepted the legitimacy of the island's present relationship with the United States; their electoral support has remained small. Support for pro-statehood candidates rose from 12 percent of the vote in 1952 to 48 percent in 1976; they have won three of the last four gubernatorial elections. More significantly, the number of Puerto Ricans who endorse the view that only as the 51st state of the Union can Puerto Ricans achieve full equality as U.S. citizens has been growing. And even the Popular Democratic party, under whose aegis Commonwealth status came into being, is increasingly frustrated by the repeated unwillingness of the United States to clarify and strengthen the relationship and grant Puerto Rico greater powers and control over its own affairs.

Within the United States, the emergence of Hispanics as an increasingly significant political force—perhaps the single largest ethnic minority by the year 2000—comes at a time when the Puerto Rican and the U.S. electoral systems are becoming more closely intertwined. Although Puerto Ricans do not vote in presidential elections, over 800,000 participated in the first presidential primaries held in Puerto Rico in 1980. Puerto Rico may send 80 delegates to the 1988 National Democratic Convention, which would make it the 13th largest delegation. Puerto Rico is thus moving irrevocably into the mainstream of American party politics with a swiftness few observers would have predicted as recently as 1975. This raises the possibility that the Puerto Rican question will be decided not in terms of the best interests of the United States and Puerto Rico but in terms of partisan political advantage.

The Puerto Rican economy is in critical condition. The

unemployment rate is approaching 25 percent—twice as high as in the most recession-stricken state of the Union—and the island is heavily dependent on U.S. Federal funds, which made up 38 percent of the gross national product (GNP) in 1980.

International questioning of the continued U.S. presence and control of Puerto Rico has been gathering momentum since 1972. From the United Nations General Assembly to the Non-Aligned Movement summits, from the Socialist International to the Conference of Latin American Political Parties, the voices supporting independence for Puerto Rico have been growing louder. The United States has been put on the defensive, and Washington has wasted considerable diplomatic capital in its annual effort to win support in the UN on the Puerto Rico issue.

This study will examine some of the critical issues that will affect the resolution of the Puerto Rican question. Chapter 1 provides a historical overview of U.S.-Puerto Rican relations. Chapter 2 focuses on the emergence of the Commonwealth, and the political and social developments on the island over the past three decades. The Puerto Rican economy, its evolution and current problems are analyzed in Chapter 3. Chapter 4 covers the international dimensions of the Puerto Rican question. The fifth and final chapter includes an examination of several critical issues in U.S.-Puerto Rican relations, in an effort to find a way out of Puerto Rico's quandary.

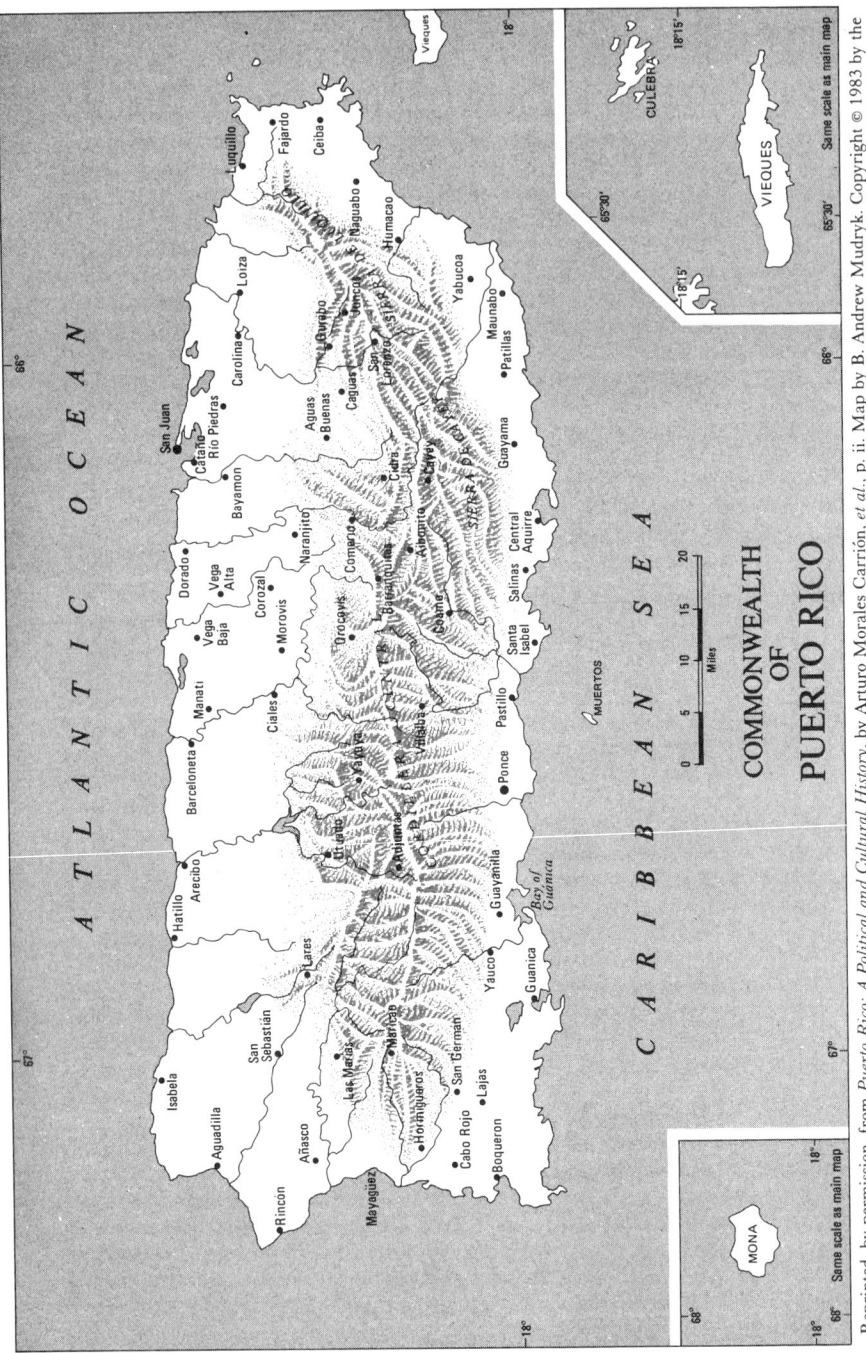

Reprinted, by permission, from *Puerto Rico: A Political and Cultural History*, by Arturo Morales Carrión, *et al.*, p. ii. Map by B. Andrew Mudryk. Copyright © 1983 by the American Association for State and Local History.

1

From Guánica to the New Deal

The Spanish-American War, that "splendid little war" in Secretary of State John Hay's words, started on April 25, 1898. In early May, the U.S. Navy bombarded San Juan, inflicting some 100 casualties. On July 25, U.S. troops landed in Guánica, on Puerto Rico's southwest coast. In less than two weeks Spain had surrendered, and Puerto Rico passed from an empire that had become a mere shadow of its former self into the hands of an emergent world power.

In many ways it was the culmination of a long-standing U.S. interest in Puerto Rico. As early as 1825 Secretary of State Henry Clay had written to the Spanish government recommending that Spain make peace with the new Latin American republics so as not to jeopardize continued Spanish control over Cuba and Puerto Rico and the islands' trade with the United States. By 1830, Puerto Rico was sending almost half its exports—mostly sugar—to the United States. The proportion rose to slightly more than half in 1860—compared with 6 percent to Spain. At the same time Puerto Rico was buying one fourth of its imports from the United States. U.S. interests in Puerto Rico were not limited to securing and broadening the market for U.S. goods; military and strategic considerations were also very significant. America's foremost 19th century naval strategist, Captain A.T. Mahan, wrote that Puerto Rico would make an excellent coaling station for the U.S. Navy; moreover, it could well become to the Panama Canal what Malta was to the Suez Canal: a key base from which to protect access to the waterway in time of war.

Colonialism with a Human Face

Except for brief skirmishes between U.S. troops and bands of rebels, Americans were well received. General Nelson A. Miles' proclamation that he had come "to bestow upon you the immunities and blessings of the liberal institutions of our government" raised the hopes of the local elite, many of whose members had long admired U.S. democracy.

Their hopes were disappointed. The relatively liberal Autonomy Charter granted by Spain to Puerto Rico in 1897, which provided a significant measure of self-government to the island, including the right to enter into commercial treaties with foreign countries, was replaced by more traditional colonial rule. A military government under the supervision of the U.S. War Department ruled the island from 1898 to 1900.

With American ingenuity and a "can do" attitude, colonial authorities set out to improve the island's quality of life. Malaria, tuberculosis and bilharzia were brought under control. A road-building program speeded travel. Americanization of Puerto Ricans through the school system was a high priority, and English became the language of instruction. Protestant missionaries went to Puerto Rico from all over the United States, challenging the hold of Catholicism.

American businessmen and corporations, meanwhile, lobbied for advantages in Washington, where the relationship between the United States and its newly acquired overseas possession was discussed with fervor. The debate on the meaning of democracy and empire engulfed the nation. At Yale University, which took up the anti-imperialist cause, Elmer B. Adams argued that "There is certainly no power given by the Constitution to the Federal government to establish or maintain colonies," and his colleague William G. Sumner concluded: "The question of imperialism, then, is the question whether we are going to give the lie to the origin of our own national existence by establishing a colonial system." At Harvard University, which sided with the imperialists, Judge Simeon Baldwin asked whether "the ignorant and lawless brigands that infest Puerto Rico" deserved to become citizens of a state or "whether Puerto Rico can be held permanently and avowedly as a colonial dependence."

The dilemma was posed in forthright terms. If the United States was to become an imperial power, it could hold colonies for a long time without any moral restraints. If, however, the nation was to be true to its origin, it had to decide to make its new acquisitions equal as states within the Union or grant them independence. Abbott Lawrence Lowell, writing in the *Harvard Law Review,* proposed a "third way," which transformed the problem into the solution. He set forth a legal distinction between different types of territories; the newly acquired territories could thus be classified as "appurtenant to but not part of" the United States. They were subsequently described as underlined unincorporated territories, which obviated the need for a firm promise of eventual incorporation into the Union, as had been the case with all previously acquired territories. Since 1901, when the U.S. Supreme Court heard the Insular Cases and adopted Lowell's definition, Puerto Rico has belonged to but has not been a part of the United States.

Foraker and Jones

The Foraker Act, passed by Congress in 1900, laid the groundwork for continued U.S. commercial expansion in Puerto Rico. The peso, the Spanish currency then being used on the island, was replaced by the dollar, at 60 percent of its value. Puerto Rico was included in the American tariff system, which meant that island products had free access to the U.S. market. This proved crucial for the rapidly expanding sugar production; between 1896 and 1940 sugar output grew 17-fold. Puerto Rican coffee production, on the other hand, the island's main export crop in 1898, which was sold mainly to Europe, declined.

The Foraker Act also granted Puerto Ricans the right to elect their mayors and the members of the lower house of the Legislative Assembly. True political power, however, rested in the island's executive branch and in the upper house, whose members were appointed by the U.S. War Department and The White House. Literacy and property-owning requirements further limited the size of the electorate. Only one out of eight people in 1900 was a registered voter.

In 1909, Puerto Rico faced its first crisis. The Unionist party deadlocked the legislature by refusing to approve the governor's budget. With unkind words for the Puerto Ricans' "lack of gratitude," President William Howard Taft amended the Foraker Act: in the future, whenever the legislature refused to approve the governor's budget, the previous year's budget would go into effect. Despite the amendment, the Foraker Act did not impose tight enough control on the local elite. Congress started deliberations on a new "omnibus bill" for Puerto Rico, and the island was placed under the Bureau of Insular Affairs in the War Department.

With the election of Woodrow Wilson to the presidency in 1912, the Democrats came to power and had their first opportunity to deal with Puerto Rico. Their view of the relationship differed from the Republican approach. Republicans emphasized territoriality while Democrats spoke of the rights of residents, and in 1917 they passed the Jones Act granting American citizenship to Puerto Ricans. With U.S. entry into World War I, Puerto Ricans were also subject to the military draft.

In addition to granting citizenship, the Jones Act provided somewhat greater room for local participation in political decisionmaking by establishing a fully elected bicameral legislature. The governor, the auditor, the commissioner of education and the attorney general continued to be appointed by the President, as were the members of Puerto Rico's Supreme Court, but the rest of the Cabinet were subject to approval by the legislature.

Puerto Rico was thus ruled by a presidentially appointed colonial bureaucracy which maintained an uneasy relationship with Puerto Rico's political elite.

Sweet and Sour: The Imperatives of Sugar

Although sugar had been one of the main cash crops in 19th-century Puerto Rico, during the last third of the century sugar producers had faced serious difficulties. Technological progress had revolutionized the industry, but Puerto Rican producers had not kept up. They thus became noncompetitive in a growing world market. But once Puerto Rico gained unrestricted access to the U.S. market, things changed. With a seemingly inexhaustible demand for sugar and sugar products in the United States, American investors quickly sensed the profits to be made. Four American-owned corporations—Aguirre, South Puerto Rico Sugar, United Puerto Rico Sugar, and Fajardo Sugar—promptly took advantage of the tight credit policies established by the colonial administration to buy land, consolidate sugar production and modernize equipment and technology.

Sugar-planted acreage increased fourfold between 1899 and the 1930s. Modern sugar mills could process vast amounts of sugarcane rapidly, and new varieties of sugarcane and fertilizing techniques tripled yields per acre. Production increased from under 100,000 tons per year in the 1890s to over 1 million tons by the 1940s. "Sugar thus became the foundation on which the island's economic structure [was] based," as economist Harvey Perloff has pointed out. By 1940 the sugar industry accounted for 20 percent of Puerto Rico's GNP, 40 percent of total employment, and 21 percent of the total amount of salaries and wages paid on the island. It also accounted for 62 percent of all exports (1936–40).

Much of the growth that took place in Puerto Rico during the first three decades of the 20th century was thus based on the rapid expansion of the sugar industry. Despite the dynamic role it played in Puerto Rico's growth, the sugar industry was by no means an unmixed blessing. It paid the highest salaries in agriculture, but it did so only at harvest time, from January to June. Most sugar workers were unemployed at least half the year, and lived under deplorable conditions. Moreover, sugar cultivation in Puerto Rico brought with it all of the negative effects of absentee land ownership, with American corporations

Figure 1.

ELECTIONS IN PUERTO RICO, 1902-1980

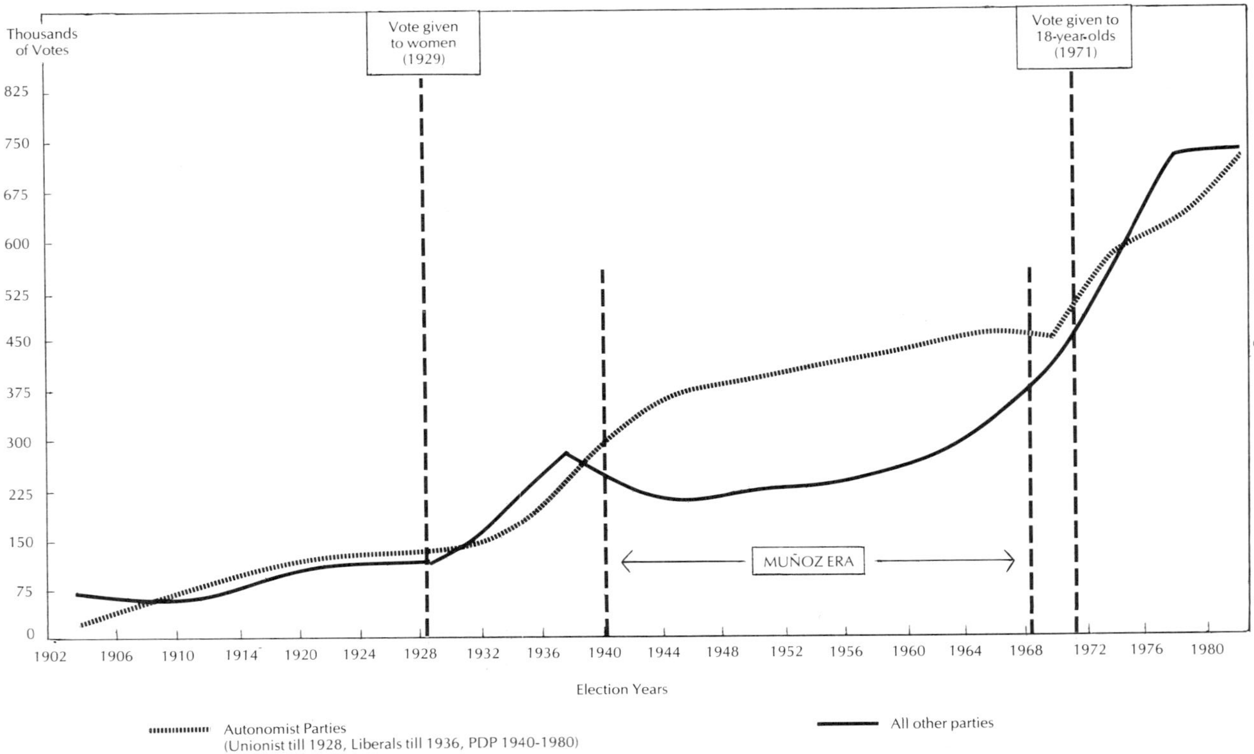

Source: Juan Manuel García-Passalacqua.

.... Autonomist Parties
(Unionist till 1928, Liberals till 1936, PDP 1940-1980)

———— All other parties

controlling Puerto Rico's best land and exercising enormous economic and political control over island affairs.

With the *hacendados,* the large landowners, unable to compete with the modern, capitalist plantation system that emerged, many sharecroppers were forced to leave the relative security and predictability of life on the haciendas to move to the cities or become hired hands to cut sugarcane.

Most significantly, sugar production locked Puerto Rico into a situation in which the island's core economic activity depended to a considerable degree on political decisions made in Washington. This fact was driven home when sugar-production quotas were imposed in 1934. They led to a 35 percent drop in sugar production the following year and the loss of 15,000 jobs.

Sugar, then, became not only Puerto Rico's dominant crop on the coastal lands from Aguadilla to Fajardo; it also transformed Puerto Rico's social structure and the nature of politics.

Political Parties and Class Alignments

The Unionist party won every election from 1904 to 1924 (see Figure 1, p. 12). The party leader until his death in 1916 was Luis Muñoz Rivera, who had negotiated the Autonomy Charter with Spain in the 1890s. The party had the strong support of the local hacendados and of a small rural middle class. It had flirted briefly with the possibility of trying to make Puerto Rico a state of the Union and felt cheated when the newly emerging economic structure favored American capital. It rebelled via the ballot box and had the support of the handful of property owners.

The various social classes developed very different attitudes toward the United States, as sociologist Angel Quintero Rivera has perceptively analyzed. Professionals, laborers and artisans admired the civil liberties existing in the United States, freedoms that the hacendados were reluctant to grant in Puerto Rico. White-collar workers in the sugar companies, merchants benefiting from increased trade with the United States, and professionals favored statehood. Many blacks and mulattoes, who lived mostly on the coastal plains and in the cities, also tended to think that under U.S. rule they would have a better chance of making it than as citizens of an independent republic or even of a more autonomous territory, where the white hacendado elite could rule unfettered by U.S. laws.

The rural proletariat, on the other hand, looked to the Socialist party, founded in 1915, to meet its needs. The party, which would play a leading role in Puerto Rican politics over the next two decades, fought for better working conditions and civil rights within the free-enterprise system. The party was influenced by the bread-and-butter trade unionism of American labor leader Samuel Gompers.

By 1920 the ruling elite was more or less evenly divided between the old hacendados and the pro-American professionals and merchants who by then had replaced the Spaniards. Each side had its own political party, the pro-autonomy Unionist party and the pro-statehood Republican party, led by a black University of Michigan-trained physician, José Celso Barbosa. The ruling parties were seriously challenged by the young Socialist party in the 1920 elections, in which close to a quarter of a million voters participated. Unionists and Republicans were pushing for greater self-government, including the right for Puerto Ricans to elect their own governor, but the strong showing of the Socialists in the elections—they obtained some 59,000 votes—made Washington leery of granting additional rights to Puerto Rico. Republicans and Unionists went to Washington in 1924 to consult with Federal authorities, and formed the Alliance, an electoral coalition, to stem the Socialist tide.

From San Felipe to the New Deal

The first three decades of American rule were a time of major social upheaval, with the emergence of a rural proletariat and the beginnings of urbanization. They were also a time of significant economic growth, with pockets of prosperity appearing throughout the island. Like a bad omen, Hurricane San Felipe hit the island on September 13, 1928, destroying almost all of Puerto Rico's coffee crop and causing serious damage throughout the island. In two years coffee production plummeted from 32 million pounds to 5 million. Shortly thereafter the Great Depression hit, and Puerto Rico was not spared. Annual per capita income dropped to $86 in 1932-33.

The economic crisis precipitated strikes and social unrest, and support for the Nationalist party, founded in 1922, grew rapidly. Its charismatic leader, Pedro Albizu Campos (who shunned the polls after a poor showing in the 1932 election), developed an islandwide following by denouncing the American presence. Political violence by the Nationalists was met by government repression, culminating in the 1937 Ponce massacre, in which the police killed 17 Nationalists who were demonstrating for independence.

In 1934, responsibility for Puerto Rican affairs was transferred to the Department of the Interior, and several members of President Franklin D. Roosevelt's brain trust took a special interest in the island. The Puerto Rican Emergency Relief Administration (PRERA), founded in 1933 to provide assistance to the island, was replaced in 1935 by the Puerto Rican Reconstruction Administration. The latter played a critical role in providing help to Puerto Ricans through a variety of economic and social programs. Some $230 million in Federal relief programs and loans were spent in Puerto Rico between 1933 and 1941.

If the late '20s and early '30s were a time of severe economic hardship in Puerto Rico, they were also a time of political progress when the common people achieved full political rights. Women who could read and write were granted the right to vote in 1929, and universal suffrage was finally established in 1936. As a result the total number of registered voters more than doubled. The combination of the rapid increase in Federal funds available for social programs and the inclusion of the common people in the political process paved the way for the rise of a new political movement in Puerto Rico.

The Birth of Populism

It was Luis Muñoz Marín, the son of former Unionist party leader Luis Muñoz Rivera, who was to play the leading role in the gestation and development of this movement. Muñoz Marín had been educated in the United States and lived there until 1930; he was a protégé of the Socialist leader Santiago Iglesias Pantín and an admirer of Albizu Campos, president of the Nationalist party. Finding a responsive chord among progressive Democrats, particularly First Lady Eleanor Roosevelt, Muñoz Marín soon became a crucial middleman between the Federal government and Puerto Rico. He played a decisive role in obtaining Federal funds—and became, in the process, the first and last Puerto Rican to exercise true influence in Washington.

Aware of the revolutionary potential of the emergence of the common people in the political arena, Muñoz Marín grew restless with old-style, elitist party politics, and in 1938 he formed a new party, the Popular Democratic party (PDP). The party's slogan was *pan, tierra y libertad* (bread, land and freedom) and its distinctive emblem, the *pava,* the peasant's straw hat. Many of Muñoz Marín's closest followers—lawyers, teachers and intellectuals—were the sons and daughters of the old landowner class, which had been displaced by the new sugar economy. Deeply disappointed by Washington's unwillingness to concede a measure of self-government to Puerto Rico and incensed by the dismal living conditions of their countrymen, they were willing to take up the fight of the Puerto Rican peasants. Muñoz Marín spent from 1938 to 1940 in the mountains in order to talk to and, in his words, "to learn from" the peasants, particularly the newly enfranchised illiterates.

It was well known that buying votes had been a regular practice in past elections. Muñoz Marín, by asking the people not to sell him their vote but to "lend it to him," won their trust. To everybody's surprise, the two-year-old PDP—Puerto Rico's first populist party—almost won the 1940 elections. In 1944 it achieved a massive victory. Working closely with former Roosevelt aide Rexford Tugwell, who was appointed governor of Puerto Rico in 1941 and was a believer in a strong and dynamic public sector, the party thus initiated an extensive program of economic, social and governmental reform. A new era began in Puerto Rico.

2

The Commonwealth: Politics and Society

"Status is not an issue" was a recurrent theme in the Popular Democratic party's electoral campaigns of 1940 and 1944. Aware that the majority of Puerto Ricans were oblivious to the perennial status question, Muñoz Marín, although himself in favor of independence, focused on bread-and-butter issues and garnered significant political support in so doing.

As World War II drew to an end, however, a changing international environment revived Puerto Ricans' interest in the issue of colonialism. The Atlantic Charter, signed by President Roosevelt and Britain's Prime Minister Winston Churchill in 1941, and the UN Charter made self-determination and self-government key principles of the postwar international order. Many *populares* pressed Muñoz Marín to start taking steps toward independence. And in Washington, Senator Millard Tydings (D-Md.) introduced a bill in 1936 and again in 1943 granting Puerto Rico's independence. In 1945 Tydings, at the suggestion of the Resident Commissioner, introduced a bill that would have offered the Puerto Ricans three status alternatives rather than one (see Table 1, column 3) in a plebiscite. Congress defeated it.

Table 1
Proposed Changes in the U.S.-Puerto Rican Relationship: The Major Issues

Years	1922	1925
Proposals	**Campbell Bill**	**La Alianza**
Internal self-government was dealt with in the 1952 Constitution. Issues in the U.S.-Puerto Rico relationship remain.	A bill creating a "dominion" relationship. Based on the Unionist party platform.	A platform proposal to create an *Estado Libre Asociado* by Unionists and Republicans.
1. Sovereignty	X	X
2. Participation in U.S. government	X	X
3. U.S. Supreme Court jurisdiction	X	X
4. Tariffs and trade		X
5. Application of Federal laws		X
6. Coastwise shipping		X
7. Banking and currency		X
8. Social welfare benefits		X
9. Commercial treaties		X
10. Foreign relations		X
11. International personality		X
12. Federal U.S. properties		
13. Citizenship		
14. Labor laws		
15. Minimum wages		
16. Specific consent		
17. Geographic description		
18. Crown properties		
19. Immigration		
20. Federal taxes		
21. Federal agencies in Puerto Rico		
22. Defense and U.S. security		
23. Full faith and credit		
24. Customs		
25. Ports and navigable waters		
26. Loyalty oath		
27. Federal District Court		
28. Military draft		
29. Territorial waters		
30. Communications		
31. Name of relationship		
32. Environmental laws		
33. Process of change		
34. Transfer of powers		

1945 Tydings-Piñero	Constitution of 1952	1953 Fernós "Cosmetic" Bill	1959 Fernós-Murray Bill	1975 New Compact
A bill proposed by Puerto Rican Resident Commissioner offering three alternatives to Puerto Rico.		A bill to clarify essential elements of the relationship after adoption of the Constitution.	A bill proposed by the Resident Commissioner to adopt "New Articles of Association."	A bill proposed by the Resident Commissioner to adopt a "New Compact" between the U.S. and P.R.
X				
X		X	X	X
			X	X
		X	X	X
		X	X	X
				X
				X
X				X
X				X
X				X
X				
X			X	
X			X	X
				X
				X
			X	X
X		X	X	
		X		X
		X		X
X			X	X
				X
			X	X
			X	X
X		X	X	X
			X	X
			X	
			X	X
				X
				X
				X
		X		X
				X
X				X
X				

Source: Jorge Heine and Juan Manuel García-Passalacqua.

Studies undertaken by the U.S. Tariff Commission concluded that if independence were granted, the Puerto Rican economy would undergo a severe depression. Statehood, on the other hand, in Senator Tydings' words, was "as far off as the North Pole." Moreover, the Puerto Rican masses, with whom Muñoz Marín had developed an extraordinary rapport, seemed skeptical of independence. In 1946 Muñoz Marín proposed a compromise solution to the status dilemma, a "third way," entitled "Pueblo Asociado de Puerto Rico" (Associated People of Puerto Rico), in which Puerto Rico would have full internal autonomy but would remain under U.S. sovereignty. Muñoz Marín's stance was denounced as a betrayal by members of the Congress for Independence, who in 1946 formed the Puerto Rican Independence party (PIP).

This third option was not Muñoz Marín's invention. Autonomy rather than independence had been the dominant goal of Puerto Rico's political elite since the 19th century under Spanish rule. As early as 1922, the Unionist party had included in its platform the goal of establishing an *Estado Libre Asociado* (associated free state or Commonwealth) in Puerto Rico, inspired by the Irish Free State (see Table 1, columns 1 and 2). Muñoz Marín, however, was the first Puerto Rican leader to obtain an effective measure of self-government for the island from the United States, to provide an ideological rationale for the emerging political formula, and to emphasize a new approach to economic and social development designed to maximize the economic advantages accruing to Puerto Ricans from the island's continued colonial condition.

Development and Social Change

Independence was aborted, but in the period 1946–52 the cause of internal self-government progressed. In 1946, after Governor Tugwell's resignation, President Harry S Truman appointed Jesus T. Piñero as the island's first Puerto Rican governor. In 1947, Congress passed a bill making the governor's position an elective one, and in 1948 Muñoz Marín became Puerto Rico's first elected governor. The most important breakthrough came with the approval of a Constitution for Puerto Rico, which came into force in 1952, after a constitutional convention, a referendum, modifications and final approval by the U.S. Congress.

At a time when most colonial empires had not yet been dismantled, the Commonwealth was widely praised as a forward-looking, innovative solution to the inherent tensions in colonial relationships. Former U.S. Supreme Court Chief Justice Earl Warren referred to it as "perhaps the most notable of American governmental experiments in our lifetime," and Harvard professor Carl Friedrich hailed it as "a new dimension in Federal government." Muñoz Marín himself elaborated on how Puerto Rico's path meant "a breakthrough from nationalism," and *The Washington Post* suggested it might be a good idea to extend the Commonwealth concept to Cuba, Panama, the rest of Central America and Venezuela.

As American investors flocked to the island, attracted by cheap labor and Federal tax exemption, Puerto Rico underwent rapid economic growth. The government of Puerto Rico took major initiatives in education, housing and health, which dramatically improved the island's quality of life. With the Popular Democratic party firmly in control and Muñoz Marín at the helm from 1948 until 1964, Puerto Rico also provided the democratic stability that seemed so sorely lacking among its Caribbean neighbors.

As a result, Puerto Rico in the '50s and early '60s became a veritable "showcase" of U.S.-sponsored economic progress and political development. The U.S. Agency for International Development (AID) brought thousands of technicians and public administrators from all over the world to observe Puerto Rico's programs and institutions. Muñoz Marín himself teamed up with President José Figueres of Costa Rica, President Rómulo Betancourt of Venezuela, and others in what was known as the Democratic Left, fighting both communism and right-wing dictators like Rafael Leonidas Trujillo of the Dominican Republic and Venezuela's Marcos Pérez Jiménez throughout the Caribbean and Central America, often in close collaboration with Washington. In the Kennedy years (1961–63), Puerto Rico was at the

Jack Delano

Left, Toa Baja, 1941: thatched huts *(bohios)* were common in Puerto Rico until the 1940s. Right, 40 years later: modern housing now dots Puerto Rico's landscape.

forefront of the Alliance for Progress. The man who directed Puerto Rico's industrialization program, Teodoro Moscoso, was appointed to head the Alliance. Former under secretary of state of Puerto Rico, Arturo Morales Carrión, became deputy assistant secretary of state for inter-American affairs, and the Peace Corps training camp was set up in Arecibo, on Puerto Rico's north coast.

A Stalemated Status

Despite all the economic and social progress taking place on the island, little changed politically in U.S.-Puerto Rican relations. From the very beginning Popular Democratic party leaders had conceived of the Commonwealth as an essentially dynamic entity that would grow and evolve with the times, allowing Puerto Ricans to assume a progressively larger share of governmental responsibilities. Numerous efforts were undertaken from 1953 on (see Table 1, column 4) to upgrade and revise Puerto Rico's status to fuller autonomy, known as a "new association" in 1959 and "a new compact" in 1975.

For its supporters, the Commonwealth was a creative, imaginative solution to the needs of a small, overpopulated island with few natural resources. While able to keep their own social and cultural identity, Puerto Ricans benefited economically and politically from association with the United States. The flexibility of the Commonwealth was one of its greatest virtues, as it did not preclude future status changes, in marked contrast to either statehood or independence, which would be irrevocable. But Commonwealthers also believed that they needed additional instruments to forge Puerto Rican progress. For example, they wanted to clarify and delimit the areas of Federal and state authority. They also wanted control over immigration of foreigners (non-U.S. citizens) into Puerto Rico, the right to set some tariffs, and full control over labor relations as well as over environmental regulations. At least three times in three decades Washington turned a deaf ear on Puerto Rico's demands, which raised serious doubts about the sincerity of the U.S. commitment to self-determination for the island.

The Popular Democratic party and its supporters nevertheless continued to maintain that Commonwealth was the best alternative for Puerto Rico. A 1967 plebiscite in favor of Commonwealth bolstered their claim.

For statehooders, represented by the New Progressive party (NPP) which has been in power since 1976, the cardinal political fact of life for Puerto Ricans is U.S. citizenship. In granting citizenship in 1917, they argue, the U.S. Congress created an unbreakable bond between the United States and all Puerto Ricans. They question the constitutionality of Commonwealth status, for which there is no precedent in American constitutional practice, and affirm that under the Constitution's territorial clause Congress continues to exercise full powers over the island. As long as Puerto Rico is not fully represented in the U.S. Congress—it has only a Resident Commissioner in the House of Representatives, without voting rights on the floor of the House—Puerto Ricans will continue to be second-class American citizens.

They are saddled with many of the duties of citizenship—they have served in the U.S. armed forces in four wars—but are unable to fully exercise the rights of U.S. citizens, including the right to vote in presidential elections. Puerto Rico's problems, they argue, will not be solved until it becomes a state of the Union.

With two senators and seven representatives, Puerto Rico would have a congressional delegation larger than half of the 50 states. This, plus the right to vote in presidential elections, would give Puerto Rico sufficient leverage within the American political system to increase the allocation of Federal funds for the island. As it is, Puerto Rico is excluded from a number of Federal programs and limited in its participation in others. The security of statehood would also enhance the island's attractiveness to investors, despite the gradual imposition of Federal taxation that would come together with statehood.

The independence parties, on the other hand, of which the largest and most significant is the Puerto Rican Independence party, argue that Puerto Rico's growth and development as a nation have been seriously impaired by U.S. colonial ties. The reason for the island's inability to solve its chronic unemployment problem is a simple one, according to *independentistas:* lack of control over its own tariffs and over monetary policy. Puerto Rico therefore is unable to develop economic policies suited to the island's needs and priorities. Commonwealth status, they maintain, is nothing but a spruced-up version of colonialism, which allows U.S. corporations to make huge tax-free profits by paying much lower wages than they would have to pay in the United States. Statehood, they claim, would be the culmination of colonialism, an act that would put in danger the very existence of the Puerto Rican nation.

The Puerto Rican Socialist party (PSP), a smaller, more radical party than the social democratic PIP, is particularly critical of the U.S. military presence in Puerto Rico. Roosevelt Roads is the largest U.S. Navy base in the world, and Vieques Island is regularly used for target practice by the Navy. The Socialists maintain that elections under current colonial conditions, in which the PIP has obtained 5 percent and the PSP less

San Juan Star photo by José Garcia
Governor Luis Muñoz Marín (left) with President Rómulo Betancourt (right) of Venezuela in February 1963. They agreed to join forces to fight communism and right-wing dictators.

than 1 percent of the vote, are meaningless. Only a full transfer of powers from the United States to Puerto Rico would allow the proper exercise of democratic rights, argue PSP members. Independentistas have also been critical of the fact that the island's colonial status has caused so many Puerto Ricans to emigrate to the United States.

Puerto Rican Migration

"The uneven equation between the unlimited fertility of the people and the limited fertility of the soil" is how *Life* magazine in 1943 somewhat uncharitably described Puerto Rico's basic problem. Indeed, Puerto Rico's population almost doubled between 1899 and 1940, to 1.87 million, a large population for an island of a mere 3,435 square miles—less than three times the size of Rhode Island, the smallest of the 50 states. Moreover, sugarcane cultivation, the island's principal economic activity, provided mostly seasonal employment, leaving long periods of idle time (*tiempo muerto*) between harvests.

Although Puerto Ricans have been free to migrate to the United States since 1917, time and expense limited the number of those traveling to the mainland. Many who made the long journey to New York City returned to Puerto Rico when economic conditions on the mainland worsened. During the early years of the Great Depression—from 1931 to 1934—a net total of 8,694 Puerto Ricans returned to the island, setting a pattern that would repeat itself.

All this changed after World War II. Cheap air fares, a strong demand for low-paid labor by the garment industry, and active promotion of migration to the United States by the Puerto Rican government led to a flood of Puerto Ricans into the sweatshops of New York City. From 1946 to 1950 net Puerto Rican migration to the United States reached 31,000 a year; in the '50s it rose to 41,000 annually. As recently as 1940, the total number of Puerto Ricans in the United States was estimated to have been a mere 70,000. Hundreds of thousands of Puerto Ricans found themselves transplanted from tranquil tropical mountain towns like Utuado and Jayuya to the very heart of the world's largest metropolis, mostly in New York's East Harlem (renamed *El Barrio*), but also in Brooklyn and the Bronx.

Puerto Rican migration slowed in the '60s, and by the early '70s had reversed itself as more and more Puerto Ricans returned home. But as a result of previous migratory waves, it is estimated that some 2 million Puerto Ricans—compared with 3.2 million living on the island—now live more or less permanently on the mainland. They are no longer so heavily concentrated in New York City; there are significant Puerto Rican communities in Philadelphia, Boston, Chicago, Newark and elsewhere.

Living in the cities' worst slums, working in the most menial jobs—if they can find employment at all—and facing harsh discrimination both because of their language and their color, Puerto Ricans in the United States have found it impossible to make the dreams that brought them from their Caribbean surroundings come true. A 1975 study, for example, found that Hispanic families in the United States had substantially lower incomes than the average U.S. family, and that among Hispanics,

Puerto Ricans had the lowest income of all, with a median of $7,629, versus $9,498 for Mexican Americans and $11,410 for Cuban Americans and other Latin Americans.

The Northeast, where most Puerto Ricans settled, was the region most heavily hit by the recessions of the '70s and the early '80s, and consequently Puerto Ricans' economic standing deteriorated even further. But their problems are not only economic; they are also political and cultural. Despite their U.S. citizenship, their large numbers and their concentrations in a few key cities, Puerto Ricans have been excluded from the political process. Even though literacy tests in English for registering to vote and other such exclusionary tools were dropped in the '60s, the number of Puerto Rican elected officials remains exceedingly small. There is only one Puerto Rican representative in the House—Robert García of the Bronx—compared with eight Mexican Americans. Maurice A. Ferré is the only Puerto Rican mayor of a large U.S. city, Miami, which has a relatively small Puerto Rican population. One important reason for this lack of political representation has been low voter turnout. Less than one third of all eligible Puerto Ricans in New York City are registered to vote, political scientist Angelo Falcón has pointed out, and the turnout in some predominantly Puerto Rican districts is often as low as 5 percent of all eligible voters. In a very fundamental sense, many Puerto Ricans on the mainland do not feel part of American society and do not feel motivated to participate in its politics. Seventy-five percent of a sampling of Puerto Rican residents in New York City in 1980, some of them born in New York, did not consider themselves American. And after all, one can still get a one-way ticket to San Juan or Aguadilla for $130....

But for those Puerto Ricans who do return to the island—particularly second- and third-generation Puerto Ricans—the transition from Hoboken, New Jersey, or New Haven, Connecticut, to Bayamón or Carolina is not an easy one. For those who are not fluent in Spanish, it can be very rough, as they are often rejected as "Newyoricans," not "real Puerto Ricans," and branded as troublemakers. Treated as "Spiks" in the United

States, as Newyoricans in Puerto Rico, mainland Puerto Ricans are the most visible victims of the division of the Puerto Rican people brought about by the massive migration programs of the '40s and '50s.

In the late '70s and early '80s Puerto Rican migration to the United States picked up again. A distinct feature of this new crop of migrants is the relatively large number of professionals and technical personnel. *Fortune* 500 corporations and Federal agencies came to Puerto Rico to recruit the cream of the crop of engineering and business school graduates of Puerto Rico's best universities in order to fill their minority hiring quotas. The quotas were originally set up to help deprived mainland Puerto Ricans and other Hispanics. In 1981, for example, over one third of the 325 engineering graduates of the University of Puerto Rico were hired to work on the mainland. Puerto Rico thus has lost some of its best talent, while mainland Puerto Ricans continue to scramble for jobs at the bottom of the ladder.

The Statehood Movement

The secret of the success of Muñoz Marín and the populares from 1940 to 1968—three decades in which the Popular Democratic party became almost synonymous with the Puerto Rican government—lay in identifying with the demands of Puerto Rico's downtrodden who had to work for eight cents an hour in 1940, who lived in miserable huts and who could not afford to send their children to school, thus perpetuating the poverty cycle. To Puerto Rico's rural population, the populares promised and delivered a different world. To this day, PDP support runs strong in those communities like Mayagüez, Salinas and others where agrarian reform took place.

Industrialization and urbanization changed Puerto Rico dramatically, bringing new issues and priorities into the political arena. Muñoz Marín understood the need to institutionalize party rule and stepped down in 1964, allowing his longtime aide, Roberto Sánchez Vilella, to win the party's nomination and be elected governor. But in 1968 there was a split in PDP ranks and the standard bearer of the New Progressive party, Luis A. Ferré, became the first pro-statehood Puerto Rican governor. Since then, only once, in 1972, have the populares won a gubernatorial election. In 1976, San Juan mayor and NPP president Carlos Romero Barceló was elected governor. He was reelected, albeit by the thinnest of margins, in 1980.

Surveys show that the typical NPP supporter tends to live in a city rather than in the countryside or one of the smaller island towns and is younger than the average PDP supporter. Even in 1980, when a majority of the municipal elections were won by the Commonwealthers, Puerto Rico's largest urban areas remained under firm NPP control. The memory of Muñoz Marín and his valiant struggles means little to Puerto Rico's younger generation, although it is still vivid in the minds of their parents and grandparents. The younger, urban population is much more receptive to the pro-statehood message. Thus, the NPP in 1976 won in all nine municipalities with the fastest population growth, mostly around metropolitan San Juan.

Important changes have also taken place in the statehood movement. It has partially shed the "100 percent American," profoundly conservative image that had marked statehooders as the party of landowners and sugarcane interests until the mid-'60s. Politically, the striving for full enjoyment of their rights as U.S. citizens, including participation in U.S. national elections, still provides the core of the statehood argument. Yet, throughout the '70s, the NPP relied more and more on economic arguments. Statehood would not only provide "security"; more importantly, it would raise the income and standard of living of the vast majority of Puerto Ricans who still found themselves below the poverty line. As a state, argued Governor Romero Barceló in his *Statehood Is for the Poor* booklet, Puerto Rico would qualify for many more Federal funds than under Commonwealth status.

The Electoral Revolt

The growth of support for the statehood movement and the relative decline of the PDP at a time of crisis in Puerto Rico's economic development, led to a fundamental realignment in Puerto Rican politics. The crucial turning point was the 1968

San Juan Star photo by José Garcia
Police evict squatters from Villa Sin Miedo in May 1982. Social tensions have been heightened by the deteriorating economic situation.

election. From a "one-party dominant" system, in some ways similar to Mexico's, Puerto Rican politics evolved into a two-party system, more similar to that of the United States. The NPP, contrary to some observers' expectations, has failed to become the dominant party. Despite a creditable economic performance during his first term and although the memories of the 1974–76 recession under PDP Governor Rafael Hernández Colón were still vivid, Governor Romero Barceló won the 1980 elections by the razor-thin margin of 3,000 votes out of over 1.6 million ballots cast. The PDP won a majority in both houses of the legislature and in most of the municipalities.

As Figure 1 indicates, Puerto Rico has thus returned to the pre-1940 pattern with two almost evenly matched electoral blocs. Then, as now, the pro-autonomy forces commanded roughly one half of the electorate, and all other parties the rest.

The emergence of this two-party system has been paralleled by a rapidly growing and more independent electorate. The total number of registered voters doubled from a little under 1 million in 1960 to over 2 million in 1980. The lowering of the voting age from 21 to 18 years of age in 1971 added almost 400,000 new voters to the rolls. Voter participation has continued at a high level—fluctuating from a low of 74 percent in 1968 to a high of 86 percent in 1976. Two of the most significant developments in the '70s were decreasing party loyalty (10 percent of the voters in 1980 split their tickets, compared with 1 percent in 1960), and the growing importance of local as opposed to islandwide issues and candidates.

The electorate was prepared to oust a governor when it did not like him; it has done so with every incumbent since 1968 with the exception of Governor Romero Barceló. The governor, however, not only lost his majority in the House and the Senate in 1980; he suffered a division in his party in 1983, with San Juan Mayor Hernán Padilla leading a Puerto Rican Renewal party.

In the early '80s, then, the consensus that had characterized Puerto Rican politics in the '50s and early '60s has been replaced by a profound division within the electorate. It is divided both as to the best course to follow to overcome Puerto Rico's serious social and economic problems and over the type of relationship Puerto Rico should have with the United States.

3

An Economy in Transition

To the tourists who fly into Isla Verde International Airport or go shopping and nightclubbing while their cruise ship awaits them in San Juan harbor, Puerto Rico must seem to be a fairly prosperous—if not downright well-off—place. There are hardly any beggars, barefoot children are nowhere to be seen, and San Juan's most serious problem seems to be the monumental traffic jams caused by the hundreds of thousands of Toyotas, Datsuns and Volvos that crowd the capital's highways at rush hour. Indeed, with a per capita income of $3,910 a year, one automobile for every three Puerto Ricans, one telephone for every four, and with four times as many jobs in manufacturing as in agriculture, the island's standard of living is far higher than that of most of its neighbors. Moreover, Puerto Rico's external trade is the fifth largest in Latin America, higher than Colombia's (with a population of 26 million) or Peru's (with 17 million).

Puerto Rico over the past decades has also made tremendous progress in health care, education and housing. The life expectancy of Puerto Ricans is roughly the same as that of mainland citizens; with one physician for every 513 people, the island can count on a large, solid core of health-care professionals. Deaths have come to reflect more and more the pattern of advanced industrialized societies, with degenerative ailments like heart disease and cancer now the leading causes, displacing earlier fatal agents like diarrhea-enteritis and tuberculosis, now almost totally eradicated.

Education has been another area of significant accomplishments; the Commonwealth government has traditionally assigned between one third and one fourth of its budget to education. In 1981 over 1 million Puerto Ricans—one out of every three people on the island—were enrolled as students. The literacy rate is 90 percent. Particularly noteworthy is the tremendous expansion of Puerto Rican universities, where student enrollment has increased by a factor of 11 over the past 30 years, reaching 135,000 students in 1982.

The quantity and quality of housing have also increased dramatically. In 1940, a full 80 percent of Puerto Rico's housing was considered inadequate; this figure was reduced to 21 percent in 1978. In 1977, three out of four Puerto Rican families owned their own homes, 93 percent of which had running water.

The Origins of Operation Bootstrap

What accounts for this dramatic progress? Until 1940 Puerto Rico was a poor colonial backwater, "our cherished slum," in the words of one American commentator. In the early '40s Muñoz Marín and the New Deal Governor Tugwell initiated a program of wide-ranging social and economic reforms which laid the foundations for modern Puerto Rico. Their best "ally" in this endeavor was Adolf Hitler. To gear up for the war he unleashed, Federal expenditures rose swiftly. Between 1940 and 1945 they grew from $59 million to $208 million, considerably increasing the meager income of Puerto Ricans. The remittances of 65,000 Puerto Rican servicemen also provided a substantial cash inflow.

In the war years a highly creative—if ideologically ambiguous—effort was made to restructure and reorient the Puerto Rican economy. With the establishment of a minimum wage, approval of a tax-reform law, and implementation of an agrarian

Table 2
Demographic Statistics

	1940	1950	1960	1970	1980
Population as of July 1 (thousands)	1,878	2,218	2,360	2,722	3,206[r]
Birthrate per 1,000 population	40.1	40.1	35.5	25.8	22.8
Infant mortality rate per each 1,000 live births	109.1	65.6	42.1	27.5	18.5
Life expectancy (years)	46	61	69	72	73

[r]Revised
Source: Puerto Rico Planning Board, *1982 Socioeconomic Statistics.*

reform program, the standard of living in Puerto Rico's lower income groups improved substantially.

An important expansion of the public sector also took place. Through the creation of numerous boards and agencies, the government started to develop the capabilities to monitor economic trends and to play an active role in the economy. The Planning Board, the Government Development Bank, the Bureau of the Budget and the Industrial Development Company were among the most significant of these bodies. The government also set up state-owned glass, cement and paper factories and took control of several public utilities.

With the end of World War II and the beginning of the cold war, however, the Popular Democratic party changed course. It moved away from populist redistribution of wealth and state ownership of industry.

Fomento's Success Story

In 1947, under the direction of Teodoro Moscoso, head of the Economic Development Administration (best known by its Spanish name Fomento), Puerto Rico launched Operation Bootstrap, a massive effort to attract U.S. capital and investors to the island.

The centerpiece of the strategy was the offer of full tax exemption from Federal, state and local taxes for those who invested in manufacturing facilities in Puerto Rico. Low wages were another key attraction. The timing was superb: there was a veritable glut of U.S. companies in search of secure outlets for their bountiful wartime earnings.

Since the demand for jobs far outstripped the possibilities available in agriculture, industrialization seemed the only road toward progress and development. Given the lack of indigenous capital and technology, the PDP's managers and technocrats decided to push to the hilt Puerto Rico's main "comparative advantage": its status as a U.S. territory. Investors were thus offered what seemed to be an unbeatable combination: low-wage environment with tax-free profits under the U.S. flag, and unrestricted access to the U.S. market.

Puerto Rico's development strategy paid off handsomely in many areas. In constant dollars, GNP tripled between 1950 and 1970, and per capita income soared, from $296 to $1,384, during the same period. Puerto Rico grew at an average rate of 6.8 percent per annum (1947–65). The chief catalysts for this growth were the hundreds of Fomento-promoted shoe, textile, clothing and chemical factories that sprang up, mostly around San Juan, but also in other parts of the island.

In the mid-'60s Federally mandated increases in Puerto Rico's

Table 3
Gross Product
(fiscal years)

Gross Product	1940	1950	1960	1970	1975	1980^r	1981^r	1982^p
In millions of dollars	287	755	1,676	4,687	7,129	11,043	12,129	12,617
In millions of constant 1954 dollars	499	879	1,473	2,901	3,422	4,149	4,174	4,011

^{r}Revised figures
^{p}Preliminary figures
Source: *Informe Económico al Gobernador 1982,* Puerto Rico Planning Board, pp. A-2, A-3.

minimum wage reduced Puerto Rico's comparative advantage. The average hourly wage in manufacturing rose from 44 cents in 1950 (31 percent of the U.S. wage) to $1.24 in 1965 (48 percent of the U.S. rate). Structural changes in the world economy also weakened Puerto Rico's position: the Kennedy Round of multilateral trade negotiations cut U.S. tariffs considerably, making it easier for foreign competitors to break into the U.S. market. This, in turn, led many U.S. companies to search for new low-labor-cost countries.

The Oil Strategy and the Oil Shock

U.S. oil import quotas set in 1954 exempted Puerto Rico. Thus the island could import cheap foreign oil, refine it and reexport it to the United States without falling under the U.S. quota system. Until the early '60s Puerto Rico used this advantage largely to satisfy its own domestic oil needs, but in the mid-'60s Puerto Rican planners realized that oil refining and petrochemicals could become catalysts for growth, replacing the apparel and footwear industries, and Fomento changed course. Although oil and petrochemicals were "polluting" industries which would create few jobs, the possibilities for expansion seemed good— from petrochemicals to plastics to the whole line of plastic-made products. Heavy investment in petrochemical and oil-refining facilities followed.

The late '60s and early '70s were "go-go" years for the Puerto Rican economy. The U.S. market appeared to be ever-expanding; the construction industry, which benefited from generous Federal Housing Administration financing, was booming; and Puerto Rico had the lion's share of the Caribbean tourist market. The average annual growth rate climbed to 8 percent and plans were made to create an "oil superport" on Puerto Rico's west coast, a symbol of the seemingly boundless optimism of the time.

The quadrupling of oil prices in 1973-74 and the ensuing recession in the United States brought Puerto Rico's economy to a screeching halt. Not only was the island overwhelmingly dependent on imported oil for its energy needs; the price differential between U.S. oil and oil produced elsewhere had become an

Jack Delano

Sun Oil refining plant in Yabucoa. Fomento's industrialization strategy (1965-73) called for refining inexpensive crude oil from Venezuela and the Middle East and reexporting it to the United States.

important ingredient in Puerto Rico's oil-refining and petrochemical development projects. In eight years (1973-80) Puerto Rico's oil bill had increased almost sevenfold to $2 billion. Since 1973 the average economic growth rate has never again reached 8 percent, and unemployment had more than doubled to 23 percent by mid-1983.

The '70s and early '80s in Puerto Rico have been a period of economic stagnation and recession. With production largely geared toward the U.S. market, any recessionary wave in the United States leads immediately to higher inventories and a slowdown of the assembly lines in Puerto Rico.

From Jeans to Pharmaceuticals: A Changing Industrial Structure

The principal reasons for Puerto Rico's economic slowdown are structural. Whereas in the '50s and '60s growth and development rested mainly on labor-intensive manufacturing, tourism

Figure 2.

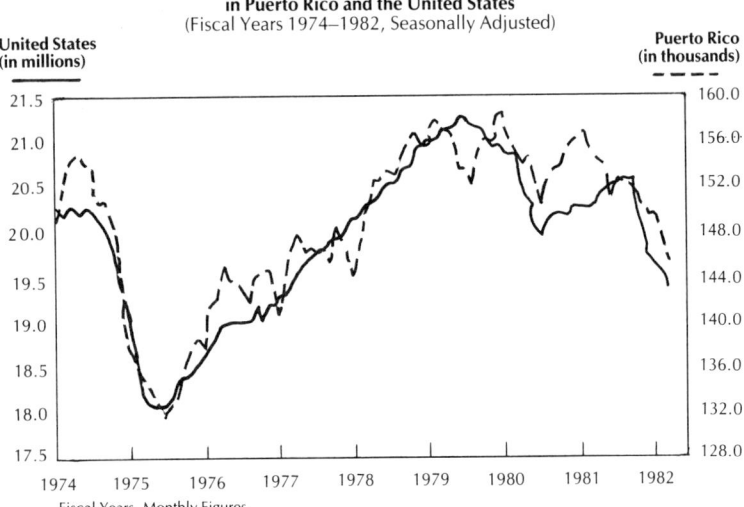

Source: Miguel Echenique, "The Economy of Puerto Rico in Fiscal 1982 as Seen Through the Determining Short-Term Variables of the Inducing Sector—Part Two." *Puerto Rico Business Review,* May 1982, p. 3.

and construction, in the '70s the most dynamic sector was capital-intensive industry—heavily export-oriented and using little local content in its products. From 1970 to 1980 the contribution of labor-intensive industries (food, tobacco products, textiles, apparel, leather products, furniture, paper products and printing, stone, clay and glass products) to total manufacturing output fell, from 63 percent to 31 percent, whereas the contribution of the capital-intensive sector (chemicals, machinery and metal products, oil, rubber and plastics) rose, from 35 percent to 67 percent. Chemical products, including pharmaceuticals, accounted for over one third of Puerto Rico's total manufacturing output in 1980.

These industries have several advantages over their more traditional counterparts: they tend to pay higher salaries, and they train workers in the use of advanced industrial equipment.

And the pharmaceutical industry, at least, has proven less vulnerable to the fluctuations of the U.S. business cycle than, say, the textile and garment industries. On the other hand, as they expand production, they create relatively few new jobs. In 1982, for example, Puerto Rico's chemical industry produced 40 percent of total manufacturing income but employed only 10.5 percent of the manufacturing labor force. The garment sector, by contrast, produced a mere 7 percent of total manufacturing income in 1980, but employed twice as many workers.

Thus, in the '70s, while GNP climbed from $4.6 billion to $11 billion, the industrial work force grew by only 25,000, half the number of jobs lost in agriculture and construction.

A Burgeoning Bureaucracy

Far and away the fastest growing sector in the '70s was government. It grew in all areas—including investment, regulation, the provision of basic services and employment. By 1980 over one fourth of the active labor force worked in government, making it the single most important employer on the island.

Because public administration in Puerto Rico is centralized, these figures include employees who would be on city or county payrolls in the States. All public schools, for example, are run by the Department of Public Instruction. The government also operates most public health care facilities. Utilities are publicly owned. But the main reason for the expansion of the public payroll has been the private sector's inability to create jobs fast enough to keep up with the rapid expansion of the labor force.

One reason Puerto Rico's bureaucracy could swell at such a fast rate was because of the availability of vast amounts of Federal funds, not only transfer payments to individuals but also grants to the state and municipal governments.

The Impact of Federal Largesse

Only a massive infusion of Federal funds saved the Puerto Rican economy from collapse in the mid-'70s (see Table 4). The most significant addition to Federal expenditures in Puerto Rico was the Food Stamp Program, introduced in 1974. In 1980, over half of Puerto Rico's families could receive food stamps.

Figure 3.

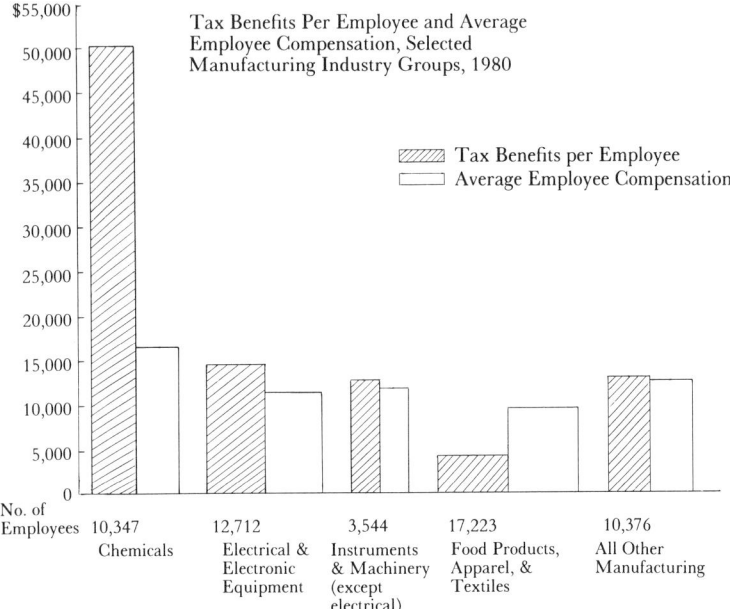

Note: The height of the bars indicates the tax benefits per employee and the average compensation per employee. Because the width of the bars indicates the number of employees, the area indicates total tax benefits and total compensation.

Source: U.S. Department of the Treasury, "The Operation and Effect of the Possessions Corporation System of Taxation." *Fourth Report*, February 1983, p. 114. Possessions corporations are companies incorporated in the United States but exempt under Section 936 of the U.S. Tax Code for Federal tax on income from operations in Puerto Rico, American Samoa or Guam. The figure shows the high tax benefits obtained by the chemical industry in Puerto Rico through Section 936. The U.S. Department of the Treasury and Congress have repeatedly tried to limit what they consider to be excessive tax benefits accruing to pharmaceutical companies in Puerto Rico. Minor restrictions were introduced in 1982.

Washington's expenditure of $10 million a day—three times as much, on a per capita basis, as current Soviet aid to Cuba—helped to keep the Puerto Rican economy afloat, but it had serious implications. These became readily apparent when President Ronald Reagan cut Federal spending. The elimination of the Comprehensive Employment and Training Act (CETA) program alone cost Puerto Rico over 25,000 jobs between February 1981 and January 1982. Federal welfare programs, with eligibility requirements set for income standards that are higher than those prevailing in Puerto Rico, have had a significant impact on the work ethic. When <u>a majority of the population</u> receives food stamps, any stigma associated with receiving a government handout is soon erased. Moreover, the incentives for not working are strengthened by a reward structure in which the differential between the monthly wage for unskilled labor and unemployment compensation-plus-food-stamps is much lower than in the United States. Furthermore, transfer payments contribute little toward Puerto Rico's long-term economic development needs, and a large amount of consumer spending goes for imported goods and finds its way right off the island.

Problems and Prospects in the 1980s

As Puerto Rico approaches the last decade of the 20th century, it faces key economic challenges. How they are approached will have a decisive impact not only on the island's economic wellbeing but also on its politics and its relationship with the United States. U.S. involvement in the Puerto Rican economy—both by the Federal government and the private sector—is widespread and pervasive. Close cooperation between Puerto Rico and the United States is therefore an imperative. Following are the most critical challenges:

- <u>High unemployment</u>

With unemployment approaching 25 percent in the early '80s, job creation is clearly the major public policy issue in Puerto Rico. Puerto Rico's unemployment is all the more severe because heads of households are strongly represented among the jobless.

Even in the boom years of the middle and late '60s, unemployment never declined below 10 percent, but the record rates of the early '80s indicate a steadily worsening situation.

High unemployment goes together with a relatively low ratio of labor-force participation, that is, the ratio of people who are working or actively looking for work vis-à-vis the total population. This ratio declined from 53 percent in 1950 to 43 percent in

1980, reaching significantly lower levels than those found, for example, in the United States, where it is around 60 percent.

- Lower investment rates

Puerto Rico's earlier extraordinary economic growth was partially achieved because of the high fixed-capital investment rate, which reached 30 percent of GNP in the early '70s. By 1979 that investment rate had declined to less than 20 percent. This occurred at a time when investment funds were more plentiful than ever: "936 funds"—those deriving from the earnings of U.S. corporations operating in Puerto Rico under Section 936 of the U.S. Tax Code—reached $8.1 billion in 1981. By law, the funds have to be reinvested in Puerto Rico. Yet the bulk of them find their way back to the United States through the Puerto Rican banking system, without being used in Puerto Rico.

Table 4
Federal Funds Received in Puerto Rico
(in millions of dollars)

	fiscal years			
	1965	1970	1975	1980
Transfer payments (social security, unemployment compensation, relief payments, etc.)	136.7	303.3	1,167.1	2,359.5
Customs duties and rum excise taxes	60.9	118.6	136.1	240.2
Expenditures of Federal agencies in Puerto Rico	110.8	160.8	188.0	302.8
Grants to the state government and municipalities	126.0	256.5	650.6	1,348.4
Total amount of funds received	434.4	839.2	2,141.8	4,250.9
Minus: payments to Federal government	109.4	231.1	591.2	834.8
Net amount of funds received	325.0	608.1	1,550.6	3,416.1
Puerto Rico gross product	2,748.0	4,687.5	7,129.5	11,031.0
Share of Federal funds of gross product (percentage)	15.8	17.9	30.0	38.5

Source: *Informe Económico al Gobernador 1982,* Puerto Rico Planning Board, p. 410.

Figure 4.

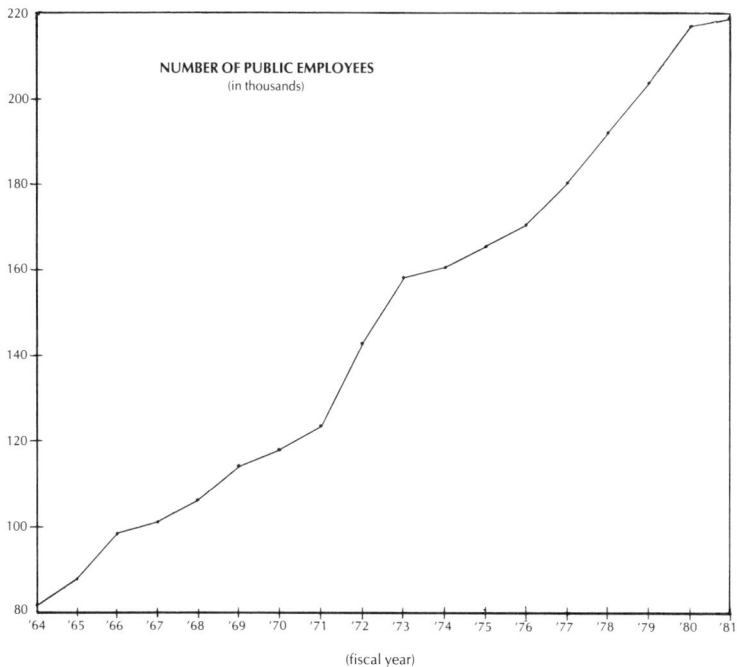

Sources: 1964–1977: *Economic Study of Puerto Rico,* Vol. I. United States Department of Commerce, Washington, D.C., 1978, p. 141.

1979–1981: Junta de Planificación de Puerto Rico, *Serie Histórica del Empleo, el Desempleo y Grupo Trabajador en Puerto Rico 1981,* p. 48.

- A negative personal savings rate

Over the past decades Puerto Ricans have not been large savers; in fact, indicators regularly show a negative personal savings rate. A variety of explanations have been offered for this—most of them related to the introduction of U.S. consumer habits into a society whose income is still less than half that of the poorest state of the Union—Mississippi. The infusion of Federal transfer payments, rather than freeing funds for savings, has only increased consumer spending.

- An excessive dependence on Federal funds

As the "Reagan revolution" has underscored, it was a mistake to bank on the continued expansion and growth of Federal social programs. Yet the $4 billion a year flowing into Puerto Rico from Federal sources have become indispensable, and the cutbacks have wreaked havoc on the island's economy.

An important part of Puerto Rico's remarkable economic performance and growth has been built on the shaky foundations of external investment, the willingness of the U.S. taxpayer to continue to subsidize Puerto Rico through Federal tax exemptions for U.S. companies, and a massive program of transfer payments. Depending, as it does, on the vagaries of U.S. public opinion and the willingness of the U.S. government to continue all or any of these policies, it is an economy operating under conditions of extreme uncertainty. There will have to be some very fundamental changes if Puerto Rico wants to preserve even a measure of the relatively high standard of living a majority of its population has come to enjoy.

Toward a New Development Strategy

Puerto Rico's economy, then, has become fundamentally oriented toward consumption rather than production, spending rather than saving, financial speculation rather than productive investment. And, instead of evolving toward greater self-sufficiency, it is becoming ever more dependent on Federal funds.

In the '40s, upon unexpectedly receiving hundreds of millions of dollars from Washington from rum excise taxes and war-related expenditures, the government undertook a major investment program in public utilities, infrastructure and industrial development facilities from which Puerto Rico benefits to this day. In the '80s, billions of Federal dollars are being spent in shopping malls rather than being invested in Puerto Rico's future. A radically new approach focusing on Puerto Rico's concrete economic problems is long overdue. Its central objective should be the creation of jobs.

Such a strategy could well be implemented in a relatively short time, but it would entail a major rethinking of the island's

Figure 5.

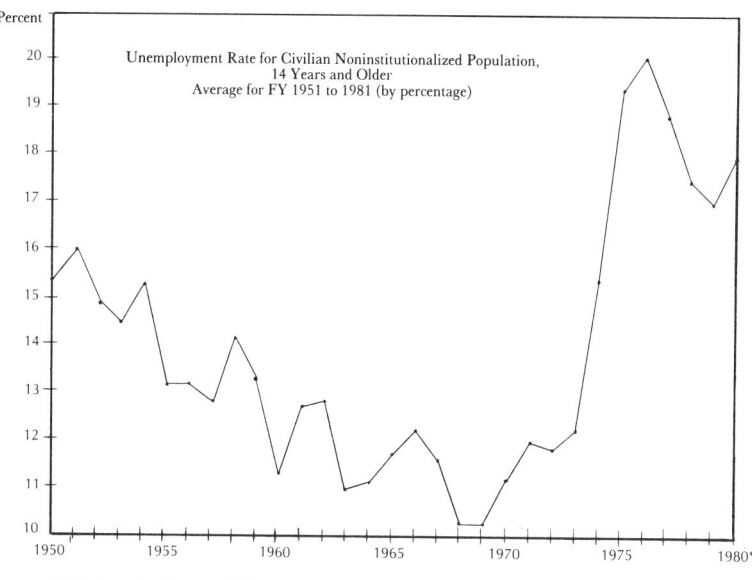

Source: Junta de Planificación de Puerto Rico, *Serie Histórica del Empleo, el Desempleo y Grupo Trabajador en Puerto Rico 1981*, p. 15.

development priorities. The following should be key components of such a strategy:

■ A tax policy that rewards savings and investment rather than consumption; an increased savings rate is critical to increase domestic investment. There is no reason why the interest paid on consumer loans, for example, should be a tax-deductible item.

■ An industrial incentives policy aimed at expanding manufacturing operations horizontally (that is, increasing interindustry linkages and use of locally produced inputs) and vertically (bringing research and development work to the island and producing more for the Puerto Rican and Caribbean markets). Unless Puerto Rico's industrialization undergoes such a "deepening" process, local plants will continue to be simply a more sophisticated version of the Mexican *maquiladoras* across the Texas border, which use duty-free U.S. imports to manufacture products for the U.S. market.

■ Agricultural and land-use policies that put an end to the unfettered expansion of residential and commercial development into agricultural land, that tax unused agricultural land at higher rates, and that guarantee viable prices for locally produced fruits, vegetables and commodities, thus making possible a healthy, dynamic agricultural sector.

■ A tourism policy that aims at spreading tourism throughout the island rather than continuing to channel it all to San Juan. Puerto Rico's west coast, for example, could well become what the north coast of Jamaica has long been and the Dominican Republic's north coast is developing into: a significant magnet for the many tourists who go to the Caribbean trying to get away from the vicissitudes of city life.

■ A public-works program aimed at reviving Puerto Rico's construction industry, a labor-intensive activity that has traditionally used a considerable amount of locally produced materials. For example, a rail system for providing the San Juan metropolitan area with the sort of mass transportation it deserves is long overdue. It is also the type of project that can help to rally the creative energies of Puerto Rican entrepreneurs, workers and public officials in a way that has not been seen since the '40s and '50s.

The costs of such an ambitious rebuilding and redirecting of the economy are not insignificant. But the resources are there. A gradual shifting of part of the Federal transfer payments program into block grants to be used for economic development projects could make available $1.5 billion to $2 billion a year. And a serious effort to ensure that "936 funds" are actually used for productive investments in Puerto Rico, rather than siphoned off to U.S. banks or used for consumer credit, would also have a dramatic effect in raising Puerto Rico's investment rate.

Puerto Rico can and should use the remarkable opportunity offered by the availability of these funds to fully mobilize the island's resources. They may not be there forever. The United States, on the other hand, should look with sympathy at efforts made to use what is ultimately U.S. taxpayers' money for long-term, self-sustaining economic development projects rather than in an ongoing shopping spree.

4

Puerto Rico on the Global Scene

If it ever was a purely domestic issue for the United States, the Puerto Rican question long ago ceased to be one. Whether the United States likes it or not, it must face the issue in a variety of international forums. Once the Cubans' pet issue to irk the United States, Puerto Rico is no longer exclusively a Cuban, third-world or Soviet issue. Consider the following:

● On September 24, 1982, the UN General Assembly rejected by 70 to 30, with 43 abstentions, a Cuban resolution to include Puerto Rico as a separate item on the Assembly's agenda for that year. A solid victory for the United States? Perhaps, but at a high cost. The United States had to use all its diplomatic muscle in a frantic, global effort to cajole countries, particularly Latin Americans, not to vote in favor of the resolution. According to more than one observer, the process was so humiliating to several governments that shortly thereafter they helped elect Nicaragua to the UN Security Council against Washington's strong opposition.

● At the March 1983 summit of the Non-Aligned Movement in New Delhi, India, the following statement was issued:

> Recalling the previous decisions of the movement and reaffirming the need to do away with colonialism in all its forms and

manifestations, the heads of state or government reiterated their support for the Puerto Rican people's inalienable right to self-determination and independence in conformity with resolution 1514(XV).

- At the April 1983 Albufera, Portugal, conference of the Socialist International, at which the political parties now ruling France, Spain, Portugal, Sweden, Greece, the Dominican Republic and other countries were represented, the final declaration stated: "The Socialist International supports the independence of Puerto Rico—a Latin American nation."

Support for Puerto Rican independence did not originate with Cuba's Premier Fidel Castro or former West German Chancellor Willy Brandt's Socialist International organization; it began with the father of Latin American independence, Simón Bolívar, who in the early 19th century led the struggle for liberating not only his native Venezuela, but also Colombia, Ecuador, Peru and Bolivia.

Puerto Rico as a Latin American Issue: The Roots

From the early stages of the Latin American independence struggle, Bolívar was interested in liberating Puerto Rico. In 1816 Venezuelan insurgent ships tried to invade the island, and six months later Bolívar himself came ashore in nearby Vieques Island before returning to Venezuela. Bolívar used the threat of a Puerto Rican invasion to try to get Washington to force Spain to make peace with him. In 1827 he wrote: "The moment has come to make the desired expedition to Havana and Puerto Rico," but, realizing England would not help him, dropped it. Bolívar kept his plan for Puerto Rican independence alive until his death in 1830.

Bolívar was not the only prominent Latin American leader to take up the cause. In the latter part of the 19th century, the founder of the Cuban nation, José Martí, worked to unite Cuban and Puerto Rican separatists in their struggle against Spain. Some of his top aides in that effort were Puerto Ricans whom he sent to Venezuela in search of support. The Martí-sponsored

Cuban Revolutionary party set as its goals the achievement of the independence of Cuba and "to foment and assist that of Puerto Rico." Thus, two of the most prominent Latin American leaders of the 19th century established a commitment in the region to Puerto Rican independence, which survives to this day.

The Origins of Internationalization

Although there was opposition in Latin America to the U.S. annexation of Puerto Rico, it was not until the 1920s that the Puerto Rican issue came to the fore again. A strong nationalist movement developed on the island for the first time, and the Nationalist party commissioned Pedro Albizu Campos, a mulatto Harvard Law School graduate from southern Puerto Rico, to visit several Latin American countries to propagate the Puerto Rican nationalist cause. He left in 1927 and returned in 1930 to be elected president of the party. On his tour he denounced "Yankee imperialism," tried to organize the groups in sympathy with Puerto Rican independence, and preached "Ibero-Americanism." In the early '50s, he was arrested for leading a nationalist uprising. The arrest met with strong adverse reaction in Latin America.

The UN, Decolonization and the Case of Puerto Rico

With the establishment of the UN in the wake of World War II, decolonization became an important principle of the emerging world order. Chapter 11 (Articles 73 and 74) of the UN Charter contains the Declaration Regarding Non-Self-Governing Territories that established the accountability of metropolitan powers for their rule over dependent territories. The United States included Puerto Rico on the List of Non-Self-Governing Territories in 1946 and reported annually on Puerto Rico's situation until 1952. In 1953, after the establishment of the Commonwealth, the State Department notified the UN that Puerto Rico's new status warranted its removal from the list, and the issue was taken up in the General Assembly's Fourth Committee, which deals with decolonization. The committee rejected a request by the president of the Puerto Rican Independence party, Gilberto

Concepción de Gracia and another by the Nationalist party to be heard on the subject.

Several countries—most prominently India, Guatemala and Mexico—expressed their satisfaction at the progress that had taken place in Puerto Rico's quest for self-government but manifested doubts that the Commonwealth of Puerto Rico, as it was established in 1952, fully complied with the world body's criteria for self-government. As the Indian delegate put it:

> ... my delegation is not convinced that Puerto Rico, under its present association with the United States, has become a self-governing territory. In our opinion, there can be no free, just or valid compact, association or agreement between two countries or territories except on a basis of equality. We believe that independence should precede any voluntary association....

Most Latin American nations, however—most prominently Brazil, Chile, Colombia, Costa Rica, Ecuador and Panama—sided with the United States. And in the November vote in the General Assembly, the resolution to drop Puerto Rico from the List of Non-Self-Governing Territories was adopted by 26 votes to 16, with 18 abstentions. The Latin American nations provided the crucial support for the U.S. position: only Mexico and Guatemala voted against the resolution, and Venezuela and Argentina abstained. As one commentator put it, power politics rather than strict legal logic carried the day.

For seven years there was little movement on the Puerto Rico issue at the UN, but with the admission of new African and Asian countries, the push for decolonization acquired a new momentum. Resolution 1514, the Declaration on the Granting of Independence to Colonial Countries and Peoples, was passed in 1960. It was to become a crucial tool for Cuban efforts to bring the case of Puerto Rico to international attention.

The Role of Revolutionary Cuba

The Cuban revolution had a strong impact in Puerto Rico, as it did throughout Latin America, and in 1959 the Movement for

Independence—predecessor of the current Puerto Rican Socialist party—was founded in San Juan. The young, radical group soon established close ties with the Cuban revolutionary government and asked to be heard by the Decolonization Committee, or Committee of 24, set up by the UN in 1960 to implement resolution 1514. The United States opposed the effort and it failed.

To counter what he saw as an emerging anticolonialist campaign directed against the United States, President John F. Kennedy prompted Muñoz Marín to hold a plebiscite. Muñoz Marín tried to use the opportunity to achieve greater autonomy for the Commonwealth, but without success. The plebiscite was finally held in 1967, with Commonwealth supporters outvoting statehooders 3 to 2 and independentistas abstaining.

Cuba brought the case of Puerto Rico before the second summit conference of the Non-Aligned Movement in Cairo in 1964, and the conference requested that the Decolonization Committee take up the issue.

It was not until 1972, after the United States and Britain had withdrawn from the UN Decolonization Committee, that Cuba achieved a major breakthrough: the committee passed a resolution proclaiming "the inalienable right of the people of Puerto Rico to self-determination and independence in accordance with General Assembly resolution 1514." The committee has discussed the case of Puerto Rico every year since then, with Cuba taking the lead in introducing resolutions and working for their approval.

In March 1975 the U.S. ambassador to the UN, John Scali, made clear that Cuba's role in the UN concerning Puerto Rico's status would be a decisive factor in evaluating the course of U.S.-Cuban relations—a warning with little deterrent effect: in September 1975, the First International Conference of Solidarity with Puerto Rican Independence was held in Havana. Secretary of State Henry A. Kissinger labeled it "an unfriendly act, since it is a totally unwarranted interference in our domestic affairs."

Up to 1976, the Puerto Rican issue at the UN was largely seen as the effort of a single nation—Cuba—to embarrass the United States. Changes of Administration in the United States and in

Puerto Rico were to bring about dramatic changes in that perception.

The Carter Administration's Policy Change

With the advent of Jimmy Carter to the presidency of the United States and the victory of a party favoring statehood in Puerto Rico, a new situation was created. The island-born advisers to candidate Carter notified The White House in early January 1977 that they would testify before the UN Committee of 24 declaring Puerto Rico a colony of the United States in hopes of starting the process of decolonization.

In April 1977, the newly elected governor, Romero Barceló, met with U.S. Ambassador to the UN Andrew Young and told him he would not defend Puerto Rico's Commonwealth status before the UN because of its "colonial vestiges." In May the U.S. State Department announced that the United States had decided to abandon the defense of the status quo. President Carter issued a proclamation on July 25, 1978, adopting "self-determination and alternative futures" (improved Commonwealth status, statehood or independence) for Puerto Rico—meaning that any of the three would be acceptable to the United States.

Another crucial breakthrough on the Puerto Rico issue at the UN was reached in 1978. No longer were Juan Mari Brás, the leader of the Puerto Rican Socialist party, and Rubén Berríos Martínez, the president of the Puerto Rican Independence party, the main speakers at the Decolonization Committee hearings. Governor Romero Barceló and former Governor Hernández Colón joined the independence leaders in testifying before the committee.

As *The Washington Post* put it:

> For the first time, virtually the whole spectrum of political opinion in Puerto Rico has appeared before a UN committee here this past week and criticized the island's Commonwealth status. All the speakers, despite their otherwise conflicting views, agreed that there are at least vestiges of colonialism in Puerto Rico's current relationship with the United States.

San Juan Star photo by Jose Feliciano.
U.S. Ambassador to the UN Jeane Kirkpatrick and Governor Carlos Romero Barceló celebrate American Independence Day in San Juan in 1982.

The Puerto Rican question at the UN had come of age and a new wave of Latin American support for Puerto Rican independence ensued. The Second International Conference of Solidarity with Puerto Rican Independence was held in Mexico City in 1979, and another in Oaxaca, Mexico, under the sponsorship of Latin American Social Democratic parties.

The Reagan Administration and the UN

President Reagan has come down on the side of statehood for Puerto Rico. But at the UN his Administration has continued to insist, as have all previous ones, that the Puerto Rico issue is a strictly domestic affair, that it stands by self-determination for Puerto Rico and that it is up to the Puerto Rican electorate to determine its future—an electorate that, so the argument goes, has shown little support in the past for the independence parties.

U.S. Ambassador to the UN Jeane Kirkpatrick has tried with mixed success to keep the Puerto Rico issue off the agendas of the Decolonization Committee and the General Assembly. In 1982, for the first time in 10 years, the case of Puerto Rico was brought before the General Assembly. Although the Assembly voted not to include it on the agenda, in the procedural debate substantive issues concerning Puerto Rico's situation were discussed.

Panama had promised to vote for inclusion of the Puerto Rican case on the Assembly agenda but changed its position, leading Vice President Jorge Illueca to state:

> Independence for Puerto Rico is one of the deferred tasks of the liberating revolution of Latin American nations ... The issue of Puerto Rico has historical roots. The fact that it was not included on this year's agenda is not a solution nor is it evidence that the problem does not exist. It would be naive to think that votes cast here for reasons of state are sanctioned by Latin American public opinion.

Mexico had also promised to vote for inclusion but, when its economic crisis erupted, it abstained. Venezuela, which voted in favor of inclusion in 1982, had this to say, in the words of Foreign Minister José Alberto Zambrano:

> Puerto Rico has constituted a special concern of the Venezuelans since the beginnings of the struggle for Latin American freedom led by our liberator Simón Bolívar. Among Venezuelans there is a deep sentiment identified with the ideal of the father of our country that Puerto Rico should be a member of the Latin American family.

The Puerto Rican question has thus come to the forefront as the last colonial issue in U.S.-Latin American relations.

5

A Way Out of the Quandary

On February 24, 1982, President Reagan unveiled before the Organization of American States one of the most significant foreign policy measures of his Administration, the Caribbean Basin Initiative (CBI). The sixth and final point of the CBI's economic program referred to Puerto Rico: "Given our special valued relationship with Puerto Rico and the U.S. Virgin Islands, we will propose special measures to ensure that they <u>also</u> (emphasis added) will benefit and prosper from this program."

The Caribbean Basin Initiative

In establishing a one-way free trade zone with the nations of the Caribbean Basin and granting a variety of tax and investment incentives for U.S. firms, the CBI (signed into law in the summer of 1983) extended to the other islands washed by the Caribbean sea some of the same benefits formerly enjoyed by Puerto Rico alone. Ironically the CBI came into being precisely at the time when Puerto Rico was undergoing its worst economic crisis since the Great Depression. By granting to the Caribbean and Central American nations almost unlimited access to the U.S. market, the CBI is likely to worsen Puerto Rico's economic plight.

A score of other measures undertaken in recent years have

seriously harmed the Puerto Rican economy or have the potential to do so in the future. The massive tax cuts—particularly in the corporate income tax—enacted in 1981 and 1982 have decreased the attractiveness of investing in Puerto Rico. The island's economic development program is tied to the ultimate tax incentive: 100 percent exemption from Federal and state taxes. Drastic reductions in Federal social programs have also hurt.

Although President Reagan is on record as favoring statehood for Puerto Rico, his policies almost seem designed to cause serious setbacks to the Puerto Rican statehood movement. This apparent paradox is not difficult to explain. The fact is that the Executive branch of the United States government is almost totally unequipped and unprepared to deal with Puerto Rico. There is no single office with responsibility for coordinating U.S. relations with Puerto Rico. A large number of Federal agencies are involved in program administration and investigative and regulatory activities on the island. But U.S. relations with Puerto Rico on a more general level fall into a gray area which is not part of the domestic or the international policymaking apparatus, a classic "inter-mestic" issue. While the State Department's Office of International Organization Affairs has filled part of this gap, there is no single office with integrated, day-to-day responsibilities to deal with Puerto Rico.

The Need for a Policy

It is not surprising then that domestic and foreign economic policies are designed and implemented with little consideration for Puerto Rico. Its basic economic structure is a very different one from that of the states of the Union: Federal tax exemption is a key development incentive; the public sector plays a decisive role in economic activities and employment; and the proportion of net income derived from Federal transfer payment programs is much higher than in the 50 states. On the other hand, Puerto Rico is in a very different position from its Caribbean neighbors: Puerto Rico is unable to set its own tariffs, enter into commercial treaties with other nations or set monetary policy.

Only a policy specifically designed for Puerto Rico will do. But

U.S. policy toward the island over the past three decades has been piecemeal and ad hoc, at best characterized by "selective inattention," at worst by "benign neglect."

Self-Determination as Evasion

"Why are you worrying about statehood and independence? . . . You will get either or both as soon as you are ready," said Congressman Joseph Cannon in an address to a joint session of the Puerto Rican legislature in an April 1919 visit to the island. The timeless nature of his words, which could have perfectly well been uttered by a visiting U.S. congressman in the early 1980s, dramatically illustrates both the continuity in U.S. "nonpolicy" and the static nature of Puerto Rico's status debate. More importantly, it fits well with the comfortable if self-serving position that U.S. officials take on the Puerto Rican question today.

In 1948, President Truman inaugurated the self-determination policy in Puerto Rico stating: "The Puerto Rican people should have the right to determine for themselves Puerto Rico's political relationship to the continental United States."

In 1953, President Dwight D. Eisenhower sent a message to the UN General Assembly, then discussing the case of Puerto Rico, saying that "if at any time the Legislative Assembly of Puerto Rico adopts a resolution in favor of more complete or even absolute independence, I will immediately therefore recommend to Congress that such independence be granted." As recently as January 12, 1982, President Reagan, in a statement reiterating his support for Puerto Rican statehood, said he recognized "the right of the Puerto Rican people to self-determination."

Who can quarrel with this position? Isn't it the most sensible and commonsensical one? Wouldn't it be a return to the crassest form of colonialism for the United States to impose unilaterally its preference on Puerto Rico's status, rather than wait for the Puerto Rican people to make up their own minds about it?

Critics see two basic problems with this line of argument. The first one arises from historical experience. It is simply not true, they say, that the United States is prepared to grant to Puerto

Ricans greater powers if they so desire. There have been at least three major attempts to revise and upgrade the present Commonwealth status (in 1953, 1959 and 1975), and all of them came to naught because of opposition within various branches of the U.S. government. One may agree or disagree with the wisdom of the political strategy followed by the government of Puerto Rico to obtain passage of the "culminated" Commonwealth bills, but the fact is that, in this respect—in projects fully supported by the Puerto Rican voters, let alone the legislature—the United States has not stood by the principle of self-determination.

In the words of Puerto Rico's Supreme Court Chief Justice José Trías Monge, "Despite the profuse expressions of the United States in favor of free determination, the truth is that, beyond the realm of rhetoric, that right has never been recognized for Puerto Rico. . . . This sad indecision on the part of the United States has greatly contributed to the prevailing chaos in Puerto Rico."

The second problem critics cite is procedural. One of the reasons there is a political stalemate on Puerto Rico's status is because the decision rests with Congress. Puerto Ricans do not know the consequences of their choosing one status option or another. All they know is that once the plebiscite is held, the U.S. Congress will decide the issue and there is no guarantee that it will accept the results, or under what conditions it will do so. These matters are central for determining support of one option over the other in the first place.

Beyond the Three-Ring Circus

In this context, then, it is easy to understand the perpetuation of Puerto Rico's status debate. The perennial exchanges on the subject tend to obfuscate rather than illuminate the issue: as Puerto Ricans engage in exceedingly abstract discussions of the comparative advantages of each status alternative—statehood, Commonwealth or independence—North Americans again and again take the comfortable position best expressed as "let Puerto Ricans reach agreement among themselves first, and then come to us." And it is precisely this attitude that has made progress in resolving the Puerto Rican question an apparently impossible task. In the name of self-determination, Washington shrugs off all responsibility for initiating change in Puerto Rico's colonial status. Yet in Puerto Rico itself, more and more the issue has become decolonization, a process that, by definition, requires an active involvement of the colonial power, in this case the United States.

All change implies some risks, and the U.S. policymakers, being what they are, would rather live with Puerto Rico's status quo than become involved in a complex process of status change. And it is true that change in the direction of the preferred alternatives of Puerto Rico's leading political parties raises not insignificant constitutional, economic, strategic and ultimately political questions within the U.S. political system.

Granting to Puerto Rico all or some of the many powers Commonwealthers have been clamoring for—say, control over immigration of foreigners (non-U.S. citizens) into Puerto Rico— raises myriad legal questions as to the rights of states versus the Federal government, as do many of the other powers (like the right to enter into commercial agreements with other nations) Commonwealthers have been asking for. The issues raised by the admission of Puerto Rico as the 51st state of the Union are not so much legal as political. Would half of the state congressional delegations be willing to vote for admission of a state that would have a larger congressional and electoral college delegation (with 9 members) than they do? Would a Spanish-speaking state with a culture that is very different from the one predominating in the United States be accepted as a full-fledged state of the Union? And what about the disruptive potential of the pro-independence minority that would continue its struggle, but this time within the Union?

The independence option raises just as many questions. Given Puerto Rico's current economic dependence on the United States, would it be able to make it on its own? How much aid would it need from Washington and for how long? What would happen to the U.S. citizenship of Puerto Ricans? And what would happen to the extensive U.S. military installations?

Even from this brief list it should be apparent that change will not be easy, and that reasonable people can differ on which of these options is the best or the least bad for the national interest of the United States. A much more productive approach for the United States would be to disengage itself from the support of substantive outcomes in the resolution of Puerto Rican status—and in this regard the July 1978 "alternative futures" policy statement of President Carter is particularly relevant. Instead it could develop a two-pronged policy toward Puerto Rico aimed at facilitating an eventual transition to any of the three preferred status options. This would mean, on the one hand, to take action on a number of very specific current problems posed by Puerto Rico's relationship with the United States, and on the other, to initiate a process leading to an eventual resolution of the status question—shelving self-determination and moving toward what political scientist Robert Pastor has called mutual determination.

What is needed, then, is an approach that responds to Puerto Rico's needs and is compatible with U.S. interests in Puerto Rico, the Caribbean, and Latin America generally. Following are some key policy areas in which relatively rapid changes could be implemented, thus easing an eventual status transition and defusing present potentially dangerous trends.

The Economic Conundrum: From Food Checks to Block Grants

As indicated in Chapter 3, despite all the progress that has taken place in Puerto Rico over the past decades, in the early '80s the island is facing some very serious economic problems. High unemployment, decreasing investment rates, a negative personal savings rate and an excessive dependence on Federal funds are some of the most critical problem areas.

There have been some imaginative efforts by the government of Puerto Rico to open up new avenues for economic activity over the past few years. Most significant have been a new emphasis on agricultural development leading to commercial rice production—a standard Puerto Rican staple—and the development of some agribusinesses using the latest cultivation techniques for

Waiting in line for food stamps in Rio Piedras. In 1982 the food stamp program was changed to an experimental food checks system.

fruits and vegetables. But, by and large, there is no overall economic development strategy. Fomento's program continues to be predicated on attracting U.S. manufacturing firms which set up assembly plants in Puerto Rico to produce for the U.S. market. Construction and tourism, the two other pillars of growth in the '50s and '60s, declined dramatically between 1970 and 1983, with the total number of hotel rooms dropping by one quarter (from 7,792 to 5,533) and the number of construction permits dropping by two thirds.

Federal assistance programs for the island have mushroomed, with gross Federal expenditures reaching over $4 billion in 1982. But these programs are mostly transfer payments to individuals rather than funds geared toward economic development, thus creating a more or less permanent dependence on the Federal purse.

Substituting half of that amount (some $2 billion) with block grants—while leaving items such as Social Security and veterans' benefits untouched—would generate considerable capital for economic development projects. Puerto Rico could use these funds to build and develop its own industrial structure, rather than depend almost exclusively on externally owned assembly plants. Investing in transport and communication with the rest of the Caribbean and helping to create industries geared to local consumption and exports to other countries in the Caribbean Basin could start to put Puerto Rico on its own economic feet. This would make the transition to any different status considerably easier. Greater economic self-sufficiency should be the goal, and job creation, the immediate objective.

U.S. Military Interests

The crisis in Central America put a halt to what had become in the '70s a steadily declining U.S. interest in the Caribbean Basin region. The October 25, 1983, U.S. invasion of Grenada confirmed Puerto Rico's military significance: U.S. naval bases in Puerto Rico played a crucial part in the operation.

In this changing politico-strategic environment, Puerto Rico, and in particular the U.S. Navy's Roosevelt Roads base located in the east, assumes a new importance as a U.S. military bastion. Because of its key location at the very center of the Caribbean archipelago, Puerto Rico has traditionally played a significant role in U.S. military strategy. It continues to do so at the present time. Although a number of military facilities were closed during the '70s—notably Ramey Air Force Base in 1973-some of them are being reconditioned and prepared to be used again. With the loss of full U.S. control over the Panama Canal, some argue that Puerto Rico's role has become more crucial than ever for U.S. naval interests in the Caribbean.

This raises a critical issue. As the Status Commission Report of 1966 pointed out, the presence of the branches of the U.S. Armed Forces in Puerto Rico suffers from a weak legal basis. The argument has been made that the Puerto Rican legislature gave a "generic consent" to their presence in a 1952 legislative resolution. However, the issue of the legal basis for U.S. military installations in Puerto Rico remains to be settled.

The case of Vieques Island, Puerto Rico's Gibraltar, is the most prominent. A relatively small (51 square miles) island located some seven miles east of Puerto Rico, it has been taken over almost entirely by the U.S. Navy since 1941: 22,000 of its 34,000 acres are under the control of the U.S. Marine Corps and the Navy. Since the Navy's takeover and consequent curtailment of many of the island's economic activities, the population declined from over 11,000 in 1940 to 7,700 in 1970 despite considerable population growth in Puerto Rico.

The Navy considers Vieques Island to be the only place where the Atlantic Fleet can undertake the full range of weapons-training exercises under simulated combat conditions—although, with the range of uninhabited islands available in the Caribbean, that seems a questionable proposition. Not surprisingly, Vieques Island is the one place in Puerto Rico where there are friction and confrontations between U.S. military personnel and Puerto Ricans. Vieques Island fishermen are irked by the Navy's restricting their fishing areas; Marines get into regular brawls with Viequenses; and economic development of the island—be it through agriculture or tourism—has been effectively halted by having two thirds of the island's territory under the control of the U.S. Navy.

Governor Romero Barceló filed suit in 1978 to enjoin the Navy from using Vieques Island for weapons-training purposes, to no avail. The Navy's continued use remains a sore point to Puerto Ricans of all ideological stripes.

In October 1983, two weeks before the U.S. invasion of Grenada, the government of Puerto Rico and the U.S. Navy signed an agreement whereby the Navy agreed to try to attract military contractors to set up factories in Vieques Island and thus alleviate unemployment. In any future status transition, the issue of Vieques Island together with the continued operation of all U.S. military installations in Puerto Rico will be raised. One of the single most important steps that the United States could take to indicate its commitment to the principle of self-determination is to face squarely, and clarify by mutual agreement, its military presence in Puerto Rico.

United Press International Photos, Roso Sabalones
A Vieques fisherman aims his slingshot at a U.S. Navy landing boat. The U.S. naval presence is a constant source of friction with island residents.

Language and Culture

If there is any lesson to be learned from the first 50 years of the U.S. presence in Puerto Rico—and the innumerable efforts to Americanize Puerto Ricans by making English the official language—it is that Spanish is there to stay and will continue to be Puerto Rico's language. On this point there are no differences among the various political parties, and statehooders have repeatedly stated that Spanish is not negotiable in any future transition.

Although English has long ceased to be the main language of instruction in the schools of Puerto Rico, there is one place in Puerto Rico where only English is spoken, a place where crucial decisions are made on a daily basis: the Federal U.S. District Court in San Juan. Although its judges are all Puerto Ricans, by law all of the court's proceedings have to be carried out in English. Again, this is an area where a remarkable consensus exists in Puerto Rico: it is an affront to Puerto Rican lawyers, their clients and the general public to have to use a language that is not Puerto Rico's precisely when some of the most central issues facing the island—ranging from environmental safety standards to the nature and limits of freedom of expression—are being argued.

An act of Congress making official the use of Spanish in the San Juan U.S. District Court would be one way to demonstrate that the United States is truly committed to respect Puerto Rico's vernacular language. Congressional failure to do so would indicate the opposite.

At a time when Spanish has become de facto the dominant language in many areas of the Southwest and in the barrios of the Northeast, Spanish should be accepted as a fact of life in Puerto Rico.

Toward a U.S. Policy for Puerto Rico

The Puerto Rican question is broader than the status issue; there are various areas in which measurable progress can be achieved without necessarily getting into either the substantive or procedural problems raised by status change. Good progress toward resolving the aforementioned issues would pave the way for a smoother and easier resolution of the current impasse. The following sections will deal specifically with the ways U.S. policy toward Puerto Rico can be shaped to cut through the Gordian knot of the status issue.

The Problem

Even a cursory review of U.S.-Puerto Rican relations since the establishment of the Commonwealth in 1952 indicates that the United States has followed a "policy-of-no-policy" toward the island. The numerous efforts to upgrade the Commonwealth by expanding its powers and autonomy failed not so much because they ran counter to U.S. interests or policy, but because of the absence of an overall policy toward matters Puerto Rican. Individual U.S. Executive agencies, the Congress and the judiciary have acted principally to protect their own turf. The lowest common denominator was to do nothing, in order not to disturb the bureaucratic or programmatic or legal prerogatives of the Navy, or Interior, or Treasury or Congress.

Anchoring a Policy

This absence of a policy stems from the low priority top

policymakers have given Puerto Rico as well as from the lack of any permanent office responsible for Puerto Rican affairs within the Federal government. This has made it impossible to build and develop the sort of human, organizational and informational resources needed for analysis, evaluation and diffusion of the data and knowledge available on Puerto Rico. The 1983 proposal to create a Senate Select Committee on Puerto Rico was thus an important step in the right direction. If established, it should allow for a permanent professional evaluation of the many conflicting issues emerging in U.S.-Puerto Rican relations.

With the territorial clause of the Constitution dictating the principle of government by Congress over Puerto Rico, the location of a unit on Puerto Rican affairs in the U.S. Congress is appropriate and urgent. The next step, then, is for that body to develop a policy toward the Puerto Rican question before the situation on the island deteriorates. Such a policy should be based on the following cardinal principles:

- *Make Puerto Rico economically self-sufficient.*

Low investment rates and the island's dependency on Federal funds have reached dangerous levels. A program of block grants, such as the one outlined above, should go a long way toward rebuilding Puerto Rico's economic development base. If half of the current $4 billion in Federal funds going to Puerto Rico were transferred to a 20-year entitlement program, it would enable Puerto Rico to lay the foundations for solid, self-sustaining economic growth irrespective of its political status.

- *Watch process—not substance.*

The conclusions reached by the United States-Puerto Rico Status Commission in 1966, that any of the three status alternatives is equally acceptable to the United States, should still be valid today. U.S. political parties, the President and the Congress should disengage themselves from the business of supporting one or the other status options and commit themselves to ensuring that the process by which a decision is ultimately reached is fair and equitable to all.

- *Search for agreement by consensus—not fiat.*

Any approach toward breaking through the status stalemate

must be fully bipartisan, encompass all three branches of the Federal government and involve all Puerto Rican political parties. A true process of mutual determination can only succeed if all relevant actors are involved, including the international community represented by observers from the UN for any plebiscite to be held in the future.

- *Make a plebiscite an end result, not a starting point.*

After a period in which Puerto Rico has started the long road toward greater economic self-sufficiency and away from the single-minded integration with the U.S. economy that has characterized the development strategy over the past four decades, a bipartisan, bilateral, U.S.-Puerto Rican process should be initiated. It would formulate, with extensive congressional and Executive-branch consultation and input, the conditions under which statehood, independence or a "culminated" Commonwealth would be acceptable to the U.S. Congress.

This would overcome the most serious obstacle to any plebiscite on the status issue in the present circumstances: Voters in Puerto Rico today simply do not know under what conditions each of the status alternatives will be implemented. A punitive independence is likely to be as unacceptable to Puerto Ricans as a powerless Commonwealth or an "all-American" statehood in which English became the official language and Federal taxes were imposed swiftly and curtly.

Once the conditions attached to each status option are clearly spelled out, the Puerto Rican electorate can begin to determine the nature of the relationship Puerto Rico is to have with the United States.

The United States needs to formulate a policy on Puerto Rico. In its design, it should heed the advice of the main character in *Macho Camacho's Beat,* Puerto Rico's most popular novel, who favors "those lyrics that speak truths, those lyrics that speak realities, those lyrics that speak of things the way they are and not the way you want them to be."

Talking It Over
A Note for Students and Discussion Groups

This issue of the HEADLINE SERIES, like its predecessors, is published for every serious reader, specialized or not, who takes an interest in the subject. Many of our readers will be in classrooms, seminars or community discussion groups. Particularly with them in mind, we present below some discussion questions—suggested as a starting point only—and references for further reading.

Discussion Questions

In what ways, if any, are the turn-of-the-century debates in American society between the "imperialists" and the "anti-imperialists" relevant to the contemporary relationship of the United States with its overseas territories?

The Commonwealth of Puerto Rico was widely hailed in the '50s as an imaginative and forward-looking entity. Today there is widespread dissatisfaction with its condition. What happened?

What were the reasons behind the success of Puerto Rico's industrialization strategy from the late '40s to the mid-'60s?

The case of Puerto Rico seems to pose an intractable conflict between the U.S. interpretation of the principle of self-determination, on the one hand, and the principle of decolonization on the other. In what ways can this conflict be resolved?

Discuss the following proposition: Even if the UN General Assembly were to approve a resolution calling for a decolonization process in Puerto Rico, the United States should do nothing until Puerto Rican voters themselves have manifested their desire for changes in the present U.S.-Puerto Rico relationship.

Should the United States help to promote Puerto Rico's economic self-sufficiency? If so, for what reasons and in what ways?

READING LIST

Berriós, Rubén, "Independence for Puerto Rico: The Only Solution." *Foreign Affairs*, April 1977. A statement by Puerto Rico's leading pro-independence advocate.

Bhana, Surendra, *The United States and the Development of the Puerto Rican Status Question, 1936–1968*. Lawrence, Kan., University of Kansas Press, 1975. A richly documented study of U.S. policy toward Puerto Rico in that period.

Bonilla, Frank, and Campos, Ricardo, "A Wealth of Poor: Puerto Ricans in the New Economic Order." *Daedalus*, Spring 1981. A rigorous, critical piece on U.S.-Puerto Rican economic relations.

Clark, Truman, *Puerto Rico and the United States, 1917–1933*. Pittsburgh, Pa., University of Pittsburgh Press, 1975. A well-rounded history of a much-neglected but decisive era in U.S.-Puerto Rican relations.

Domínguez, Virginia R., and Domínguez, Jorge I., "The Caribbean: Its Implications for the United States." HEADLINE SERIES 253. New York, Foreign Policy Association, February 1981. History and politics of the Caribbean area.

García-Passalacqua, Juan M., *Puerto Rico: Equality and Freedom at Issue in the Caribbean.* New York, Praeger, 1984. Analysis of Puerto Rican politics and U.S policy in the '70s and '80s.

Heine, Jorge, ed., *Time for Decision: The United States and Puerto Rico.* Lanham, Md., North-South, 1983. Comprehensive examination of key political and economic issues in U.S.-Puerto Rican relations.

Hernández Colón, Rafael, "Guiding Principles for the Development of the Commonwealth in Permanent Union with the United States of America." Testimony before the Ad Hoc Advisory Group on Puerto Rico, San Juan, Puerto Rico, April 27, 1974. A defense of Commonwealth status and its future development by former Governor Hernández Colón.

Lewis, Gordon, *Puerto Rico: Freedom and Power in the Caribbean.* New York, Monthly Review Press, 1963. A standard work on Puerto Rican history and society from a pan-Caribbean perspective.

López, Adalberto, ed., *The Puerto Ricans: Their History, Culture and Society.* Cambridge, Mass., Schenkman Publishing Company, 1980. A collection of some concise and informative essays: one third of the book is devoted to Puerto Ricans in the United States.

Morales Carrión, Arturo, *Puerto Rico: A Political and Cultural History.* New York, Norton, 1983. An excellent survey by Puerto Rico's leading historian.

Romero Barceló, Carlos, "Puerto Rico, U.S.A.: The Case for Statehood." *Foreign Affairs,* Fall 1980. Governor Romero Barceló makes his case.

Sánchez, Luis Rafael, *Macho Camacho's Beat.* New York, Pantheon, 1980. Witty, mordant novel of life in modern San Juan.

Steward, Julian H., et al., *The People of Puerto Rico: A Study in Social Anthropology.* Urbana, Ill., University of Illinois Press, 1956. A major anthropological study of Puerto Rican society in the immediate postwar period.

Tugwell, Rexford G., *The Stricken Land.* New York, Greenwood Press, 1968. Fascinating memoirs of Puerto Rico's last American governor.

U.S. Department of Commerce, *Economic Study of Puerto Rico,* 2 vols. Washington, D.C., U.S. Government Printing Office, 1979. The most comprehensive study of the Puerto Rican economy. Section on manufacturing is particularly thorough.

Wagenheim, Kal, ed., *The Puerto Ricans: A Documentary History.* New York, Praeger, 1973. Selection of documents and essays providing rich insights into Puerto Rican history.

Wells, Henry, *The Modernization of Puerto Rico.* Cambridge, Mass., Harvard University Press, 1969. The most systematic and sophisticated interpretation of the rise of Muñoz Marín and the emergence of the Commonwealth.